Praise for

THE FAMILY BANK

"*The Family Bank* is a simple guide to ensuring financial security for future generations. It's an indispensable resource for individuals wanting to leave a lasting financial legacy. It offers practical advice, strategies, and insights into preserving and responsibly managing wealth across generations. By implementing the book's guidance, readers can rest assured that their hard-earned wealth will be well preserved and utilized wisely by their children and grandchildren, ensuring a prosperous and secure future."

—Jaime Catmull, Nationally Syndicated Columnist, Host of the *Live Richer* Podcast

"I highly recommend *The Family Bank* for anyone seeking comprehensive guidance on estate planning through family banks. This insightful book emphasizes the significance of family banks in preserving and managing wealth across generations. John's expertise in the field, coupled with practical examples and actionable advice, makes this book a great resource for individuals looking to secure their family's financial future."

—David York Esq., CPA, Managing Partner of York Howell, Author of Bestsellers *Entrusted* and *The Gift of Lift*

"As an attorney and practitioner of implementing the family bank with my clients, I can honestly say that this book is the most comprehensive and straightforward book on the subject. John does a great job of explaining the complex topic and illustrating it in a way that anyone can understand and implement the family bank strategy. It is not a product or investment-driven book; it is his sincere way of trying to help as many people as possible in making a meaningful impact on future generations."

—Blake Johnson Esq., Managing Attorney of Entrusted Estate Planning Attorneys, Author of *You Can't Take It With You*

Any testimonial or endorsement shown is based on an individual's experience, may not be representative of the experience of other individuals or customers, and is no guarantee of future performance or success. No direct or indirect payment or other compensation is provided to any person for the testimonial appearing here.

The Family Bank:
The Key to Generational Wealth

by John H. Nebeker

© Copyright 2023 John H. Nebeker

ISBN 979-8-88824-030-4

All rights reserved. No part of this publication may be reproduced, stored in a retrieval system, or transmitted in any form or by any means—electronic, mechanical, photocopy, recording, or any other—except for brief quotations in printed reviews, without the prior written permission of the author.

This book is for informational purposes only. TFB Strategies LLC does not provide tax, legal or accounting advice. John H. Nebeker is a Registered Representative offering securities through NYLIFE Securities LLC (member FINRA/SIPC), a Licensed Insurance Agency, 150 W. Civic Center Dr. Ste. 600 Sandy, UT 84070, John Nebeker CA Insurance License OE83769. TFB Strategies LLC is not owned or operated by NYLIFE Securities LLC or its affiliates. The experience of the people described in this material may not be representative of the experiences of other clients. Experiences obtained by these people are not indicative of the future experiences that may be obtained by other clients.

Published by

3705 Shore Drive
Virginia Beach, VA 23455
800-435-4811
www.koehlerbooks.com

THE FAMILY BANK

THE KEY TO GENERATIONAL WEALTH

How to Combat Privilege and
Promote Accountability with Your
Family and Others

JOHN H. NEBEKER

VIRGINIA BEACH
CAPE CHARLES

Dedicated to Whitney.

All the riches in the world are nothing compared to your love.

TABLE OF CONTENTS

Foreword 3

Preface 7

Part I: The Dilemma. *What is the problem?*
    Chapter 1: The Wealth Riddle 12
    Chapter 2: Fortune or Misfortune? 22
    Chapter 3: Dilemma of the Dying 27
    Chapter 4: A Tale of Two Billionaires 39
    Chapter 5: Who Else Knows About This? 45
    Chapter 6: The Problem with Most Planning 50
    Chapter 7: What Planners Get Wrong 55

Part II: The Backdrop. *Where did it come from?*
    Chapter 8: The Borrower's Club 64
    Chapter 9: Financial Stewardship 75
    Chapter 10: The Three Spheres of Stewardship 80
    Chapter 11: Training with Tools 90
    Chapter 12: Compassionate Capitalism 94
    Chapter 13: Three Ingredients for Financial Success 97

Part III: The Solution. *Can it be solved?*
    Chapter 14: The Family Bank 103
    Chapter 15: The Trouble with Direct Loans 108
    Chapter 16: Creating the Infrastructure 112
    Chapter 17: The Bank Board 117
    Chapter 18: Laboratories of Learning 121

Part IV: The Application. *How do I do it?*
    Chapter 19: The "Quick-Start" Family Bank 132
    Chapter 20: Funding Your Bank: Where Is the Money? ... 137
    Chapter 21: Designing Your Ideal Legacy Assets 145
    Chapter 22: Implementing the Business of
    Family Banking 152
    Chapter 23: How Much Is Enough? 158

Part V: The Future. *What's next?*
    Chapter 24: Charitable Considerations 162
    Chapter 25: Weathering Financial Crises 168
    Chapter 26: An Increasing Need for Family Financing 171
    Chapter 27: Standing the Test of Time 174
    Chapter 28: The Road Ahead 177

A NEW, OLD APPROACH TO WEALTH AND ESTATE PLANNING

"New opinions are always suspected, and usually opposed, without any other reason but because they are not already common."

—*John Locke*[1]

---

1   John Locke, "Dedicatory Epistle," An Essay Concerning Human Understanding, 1690.

FOREWORD
A TALE OF TWO FAMILIES

IMAGINE TWO FAMILIES. The Smiths were fortunate enough to enjoy substantial wealth. The patriarch and matriarch of the Smith family, Richard and Phoebe Smith, were self-made people who believed in providing the best for their children. However, their way of doing so resulted in a culture of entitlement rather than responsibility. The Smith children grew up enjoying their wealth without understanding its value or the work that led to its creation.

As the Smith children grew older, they became accustomed to a lifestyle they didn't earn. They spent extravagantly, took unwise risks, and treated the family's wealth as an inexhaustible resource. The Smiths failed to communicate effectively about their wealth. They grew apart, their relationships marred by resentments and conflicts over money.

Over time, the Smith family's fortune began to dwindle. Their reckless spending, poor investments, and lack of unity ate into their wealth, leaving them in financial turmoil. The once prestigious Smith name became a cautionary tale about the pitfalls of uncontrolled wealth and entitlement.

The Harrison family, headed by the wise and astute patriarch and matriarch, Thomas and Jennifer Harrison, believed in a concept known as the "Family Bank." The Family Bank was not a physical institution but a strategic framework for managing the family wealth and nurturing family values. It was designed to steward the family's financial resources, foster shared decision-making, and encourage intergenerational education around money and values.

From a young age, the Harrison children were involved in family meetings discussing investments, philanthropy, and family business matters. They were taught the value of money, the importance of wise investments, and the responsibilities that come with wealth. The Family Bank not only provided financial security but also served as a platform for instilling values like diligence, responsibility, and a sense of unity.

As the generations passed, the Harrisons continued to thrive, building upon their wealth while also contributing significantly to society through philanthropy. Despite the inevitable disputes, the Family Bank served as a constant reminder of their shared goals and values, which helped them to resolve differences and ensure the continued prosperity of their family.

The tale of the Harrisons and the Smiths serves as a stark reminder of the importance of wise wealth management and the reinforcement of family values. While wealth can provide comfort and opportunities, without the right strategies and principles in place, it can also lead to disunity and financial downfall.

The Family Bank, as demonstrated by the Harrison family, is a strategic approach that helps wealthy families manage their assets while also fostering a sense of responsibility, shared decision-making, and unity among family members. It serves as a safeguard against the potential pitfalls of wealth, ensuring the prosperity of the family for generations to come.

*

Due to my long-standing relationship with John Nebeker and my admiration for his undiluted passion for the unique perspective this book offers, I am honored to write the foreword for Nebeker's seminal work, *The Family Bank: The Key to Generational Wealth*.

The Family Bank: The Key to Generational Wealth is not just a book about finance; it is a guide to altering the trajectory of one's familial wealth and securing a prosperous legacy for generations. Nebeker has crafted this book to equip individuals and families with the tools and strategies they need to create and manage a Family Bank— a powerful concept that redefines our understanding of generational wealth.

This book ventures into the heart of family wealth creation and management, dissecting the concept of the Family Bank with precision and clarity. It explores topics like strategic estate planning, prudent investment, and the power of education in wealth preservation. Each chapter is a treasure trove of insights, backed by Nebeker's decades of experience in the financial realm.

Nebeker's credentials speak volumes about his authority on this subject. A seasoned financial professional, his passion for empowering families to create lasting legacies of wealth shines through in every page of this book.

What sets *The Family Bank: The Key to Generational Wealth* apart is its innovative and holistic approach to family wealth. Nebeker does not just offer financial guidance; he offers a way of life, a paradigm shift that encourages readers to view wealth as not just an individual pursuit but a familial responsibility. This perspective is, in my opinion, an invaluable addition to the discourse on wealth creation and management.

Reflecting on my own journey, I understand the importance of focusing on what truly matters and making disciplined choices. This book resonates with that principle. Nebeker's approach to managing family wealth is not about amassing money for the sake of it; it's about prioritizing what is essential for a family's financial health and stability across generations.

I encourage you to immerse yourself in this book, absorb its wisdom, and use it as a catalyst for change. This is more than a book; it's a guide to transforming your family's financial future.

As you journey through these pages, I hope you feel inspired and equipped to create your Family Bank.

In conclusion, *The Family Bank: The Key to Generational Wealth* is an enlightening read that will change how you perceive and handle family wealth. As you delve into its pages, you'll find a pathway to creating a legacy that extends beyond mere financial wealth. I trust that Nebeker's book will empower you, as it has empowered me, to make choices today that will enrich your family for generations to come.

—Greg McKeown,
podcaster and author of the *New York Times* bestsellers
Essentialism and *Effortless*

Any testimonial or endorsement shown is based on an individual's experience and may not be representative of the experience of other individuals or customers; is no guarantee of future performance or success. No direct or indirect payment or other compensation is provided to any person for the testimonial appearing here. The author of this foreword is a family member and client.

PREFACE

THANK YOU FOR taking the opportunity to read this book. Below are some introspective questions to consider in preparation for what follows. I invite you to write your answers on each line or at least pause and ponder each question for a moment before moving on. Your reading will be more meaningful if you do. Thank you.

What is your life's work?

_____
_____
_____
_____

How are you accomplishing this work?

_____
_____
_____
_____

What remains for you to accomplish this work?

_____
_____
_____
_____

Would you like your life's work to continue after you're gone?

_____
_____
_____

If so, how are you ensuring that it will continue?

_____
_____
_____

Would you like to be remembered as someone who helped others? If so, how?

_____
_____
_____

Whom do you want to help the most?

_____
_____
_____

What are the best ways to help them?

_____
_____
_____

Of your family members and friends, whom do you think about the most?

_____
_____
_____

What is their life's work?

_____
_____
_____

How are they accomplishing their work?

_____
_____
_____

What help do they need to accomplish their work?

_____
_____
_____

How do you feel about them enduring the challenges you've experienced?

_____
_____
_____

What do you plan to do with any leftover wealth or money when you're gone?

_____
_____
_____

What would you like to see happen with your leftover wealth or money?

_____
_____
_____

Are all of your family and loved ones financially responsible?

_____
_____
_____

What are the risks of giving your money away to family, friends, and charities?

_____
_____
_____

What if, instead of a one-time gift, your wealth could benefit family and charities every year, forever?

_____
_____
_____
_____

What if your wealth could grow perpetually and bless the lives of thousands, even millions?

_____
_____
_____
_____

How can you make sure that happens?

_____
_____
_____
_____

What are you willing to do to make it happen?

_____
_____
_____
_____

1.
THE WEALTH RIDDLE

"Anyone who isn't confused doesn't really understand the situation."

—Edward R. Murrow[2]

I'VE BEEN THINKING about you. You've done well. Yes, you're still working dutifully and growing your wealth, but you've already achieved remarkable success. You've made some mistakes and endured painful challenges along the way, but those weren't in vain; they've helped refine you into who you are today. Your gains have been far greater than your losses. Occasionally, you step back and look at everything you have built; when you do, you realize it's incredible and complex, and you feel extremely fortunate.

You've learned a lot about how money works—how to earn it, how to save it, how to grow it, and how to protect it. You've generated a regular, sufficient income and methodically put savings aside for leaner times as well as for investment opportunities. As a result, you've reached a higher degree of financial security compared to that of your peers. While ensuring that you have enough to take care of yourself and your immediate loved ones' needs, you've generously shared your resources and knowledge with those around you.

You find yourself in a position where you'd like to use your knowledge and resources to more actively help your family

---

[2] Quoted in Walter Bryan, *The Improbable Irish* (Taplinger, 1969).

members and others. You have a lot to contribute; one of the greatest compliments you regularly receive comes when hard-working, ambitious people ask you for advice. Preferably, you'd like your loved ones to enjoy the same success you've achieved (or even greater) without all the struggles you experienced. But how can they best learn what they need to know to be successful? And how can you best use your wealth to help them?

You have hard-working children or family members who are already making their way in the world and having character-building experiences. Even though they're doing well, you're anxious for them to accomplish even greater things. You would like them to not endure as many hardships as you did. You have confidence that these loved ones would achieve even greater success with any financial resources they receive.

But you also have family members or know others who aren't as skilled with money or whose circumstances make financial gifts inappropriate. You have thought a lot about how to help them, too, and you may have even offered some of your money from time to time as a gift or loan to help them get by or purchase something beyond their means. You knew each time that it could be risky to offer them money, and a few times it did not turn out very well. There were misunderstandings and bad feelings. You know that either offering or withholding financial assistance has the potential to complicate those relationships. To your credit, you still want to help, but how?

You also know that someday you will be gone. When that happens, your family and loved ones will lose access to your financial help and advice. Someday everything you own will become the property of others, and that concerns you: you won't always be in a position to manage everything and ensure that your wealth is used properly. You have observed the loathsome "entitlement mentality" that is so pervasive in our society today, and you want no part in it. You know how money and wealth can help people, but you have also seen how it can hurt people, or rather, how people can hurt themselves with it.

You have already consulted with an attorney and other financial professionals to create plans for that inevitable transfer, but you are unsure if those plans will be followed or whether there will be unintended consequences. You would hate to see a significant portion of your wealth go to the Internal Revenue Service, get wasted by your heirs, or be the cause of future arguments between family members. The attorney probably assured you that his or her plan has provisions to prevent all that, but you've seen the plans of others fail to realize the deceased's expectations. You have personally seen families get torn apart by financial disputes *even when* there were extensive plans in place. Many people you know have made the "default" choice to eventually divide and distribute their assets into inheritances, but you don't like what some heirs have done with the money. Some have just blown it, and in some cases, the money facilitated self-destructive vices such as substance abuse and other addictions.

In their effort to try to prevent or mitigate all that, you have seen others just give most of their wealth away to charity, but you are not sure that is the best choice, either; you have seen some charities funnel a significant portion of their donations to administrative costs and only a small portion to the needy. Plus, you do not like the idea of disinheriting your family and permanently taking opportunities away from your loved ones in favor of strangers. You believe in some charitable giving, but you would prefer if your family chose to perpetually make charitable donations themselves. Ideally, your family would have the power to withhold future donations from less responsible charities as well.

So, is it possible to prevent your wealth from enabling bad behavior and instead ensure productive, virtuous behavior from any and all who receive it?

If any of this sounds familiar, then you've already encountered the "wealth riddle'" for which there doesn't seem to be a clear solution. The wealth riddle has been around for as long as there have been people and resources to gather, but it has started to hit home as you have achieved success and contemplated long-term plans for your

What is the best way to help others?

wealth and your family or loved ones. At the heart of this riddle is an altruistic question that is a credit to your thoughtfulness: "What is the *best* way to help others?" You would like to help people the right way, and you certainly do not want to facilitate any harm to them.

Most people like you have clear, systematic intentions for their wealth: to help family, loved ones, and the community. Quite a few advisors will tell you that accomplishing your goals requires spelling out rules and expectations in mind-numbing detail through a series of legal documents and financial products. There are many highly paid professionals who claim they know how to prevent or mitigate any misuse of your wealth through very sophisticated planning, but when you look at the multigenerational results of their recommendations, the same problems (or even worse ones) may have occurred. These professionals may not have done poor work, but their work is almost always based on a number of outdated traditions and default practices, such as direct gifting, that effectively undermine the original purpose of most planning.

My initial, personal introduction to the wealth riddle came in 2015 when my wife and I were preparing for a three-week overseas trip without our minor children. We were concerned about what would happen if we both perished in an accident, and we consulted an experienced estate planning attorney who helped us draft wills and a trust.

The day arrived to sign legal documents and make everything

official. After signing a few documents, I unexpectedly started feeling uncomfortable with what we had done, and I put down the pen. It made no sense to feel uneasy; weren't we acting responsibly by setting up these plans for our children in our absence? We had consulted an attorney who specialized in these matters, and this seemed like the prudent thing to do. Something was amiss, though, and I couldn't ignore it.

We could actually be causing a future problem for our children.

A thought occurred to me that we could actually be creating a future problem for our children. Since there likely would have been a residual amount of money left after the children had been raised to adulthood by their designated guardians, our children could potentially inherit large sums of money with no guidelines or supervision. I love and trust my children, but that bothered me. I turned to the attorney and asked, "What will happen with any leftover money?"

"Once they're eighteen, the kids would normally just inherit it," he said.

"Right. But we're not doing that, are we?" I asked.

"No. We're delaying any distribution until later, starting at age twenty-five. Hopefully, by then, they'll be more responsible," he responded.

My mind started to paint a future scene where my orphaned children had reached age twenty-five and were handed a check for several hundred thousand, maybe millions of dollars. How could my wife and I be sure that they were ready for that much money? Would it help them? Could it actually *hurt* them? Was dumping money on them the best thing to do? Would we be better off giving the residual to someone else, our church, or a charity?

I wasn't comfortable with the scenario and decided to further the discussion by posing a pointed question to our attorney: "Have you ever met an irresponsible twenty-five-year-old?" I asked.

Smiling, he looked up and said, "Okay, maybe thirty or thirty-five could be better."

"Have you ever met an irresponsible thirty- or thirty-five-year-old?" I asked in response.

> *Responsibility in financial matters is not a function of age.*

For that matter, one could pose the same question about forty-, fifty-, or sixty-year-olds. Responsibility in financial matters is not a function of age; it requires the proper training, tools, and experience to know how to grow wealth and use it for good. We have all met or heard of young, middle-aged, and even retired people making horrible financial decisions, and I certainly did not want my children to be harmed by something we did (or didn't do) through the plan we were setting up.

In drafting those documents, my wife and I realized that we had not made *any* plans to protect our children from themselves or facilitate their financial independence in our absence. Instead, we had essentially planned to dump a bunch of money on them at a future date. The attorney and I talked for a little while, and he agreed that there must be a better way than trying to address every possible contingency, but my wife and I still ended up signing the documents as drafted. We didn't make any changes because we didn't know any better. I wouldn't say it felt like the planning we had done was *wrong*, but I had an unsettled feeling that it wasn't the *best*.

Is there a better way?

Fortunately, a few families have figured out how to solve the wealth riddle, and we can learn about and emulate what they've done regardless of how much wealth we have. These select few have been able to avoid the inheritance curse of "shirtsleeves to shirtsleeves within three generations" that the vast majority of families experience. Indeed, when research has shown that 70 percent of inherited wealth is depleted by the second generation and 90 percent by the third,[3] families who buck the trends must be doing something special. Upon further examination, these prominent families are the exception for good reason: they don't do what everyone else does.

> *These families replaced gifts with loans, entitlements with opportunities.*

The solution? Instead of inheritances, these families wisely created their own "Family Bank" to retain certain assets for the benefit, rather than the consumption, of family members and others. Specifically, these families replaced gifts with loans, entitlements with opportunities. Some gifts and special grants were awarded in certain circumstances, but the bulk of the family's fortune was not distributed to heirs; it was made available through borrowing arrangements for productive use only, and repayment with interest was required. Descendants of these families do not own their Family's Bank in the traditional sense, but they each have access to the same, crucial financial services that banks and other institutions provide. Their Family Banks' officers properly train family members in financial matters and manage the bank's primary legacy assets that ensure its preservation and success. We will examine all these practices and the legacy assets in great detail.

These Family Banks have blessed the lives of multiple generations of descendants, and many of these banks continue to this day. You will not observe in these successful families the

---

3   https://www.nasdaq.com/articles/generational-wealth%3A-why-do-70-of-families-lose-their-wealth-in-the-2nd-generation-2018-10

same entitlement mentality that is so pervasive in our society today. No, the descendants of these families are not wealthy because of any inheritances; they have become *independently* wealthy through their own efforts and their unique access to capital. Money is not an uncomfortable topic between family members; they welcome and enjoy the discussion. Descendants are equipped with the training and tools to achieve remarkable success. Frankly, it is not a coincidence that those particular families have been so successful; the principles and practices of their Family Banks actually have *everything* to do with it.

Besides facilitating prosperity, the Family Bank also creates a bulwark against future financial crises by relying less on government or charitable sources and instead providing the liquidity that individuals and groups need to survive. Those with access to cash provided by the Family Bank can even thrive in times of crisis. Those unable to secure adequate financing through traditional sources for whatever reason have another funding option through the Family Bank.

Although this solution may sound new, some families have maintained their Family Banks for hundreds of years, and the principles undergirding them date back to ancient times. Rather than divide and diminish the strength of a family's fortune through inheritances, each successive generation actually brings more opportunities and growth to their Family's Bank.

The Family Bank is not exclusive to families with great wealth. Because the same principles of growth, protection, and opportunity apply to fortunes both large and small, families with smaller fortunes can maintain and grow their Family Banks at the same rate as

A family's small fortune can grow to match other large family fortunes over time.

larger ones. Family Bank activities are scalable and proportionate to whatever amount of wealth is set apart for continued growth and assistance toward its members and others. And by using the ideal legacy assets inside the Family Bank, a family's small fortune can grow to match other large family fortunes over time. A relatively small amount of wealth can snowball into a sizable reservoir of wealth in several generations, and family members can quickly "outgrow" their individual need for the Family Bank's services by accumulating their own financial reserves. Ideally, they will establish their own Family Banks when the time is right, and their children and their children's children will follow the same pattern.

The word must get out. There are articles in the news regularly about famous or wealthy people making planning choices with lasting consequences to their families and communities. Unfortunately, most of those plans lack the proper structure to ensure accountability and success, and their accumulated wealth is likely to be consumed in a short amount of time regardless of the amount. Each time I see a headline, I am reminded that there is a better, less common solution that most have never even heard of.

Solving the wealth riddle requires a course correction.

You'll need a course correction to solve the wealth riddle, and the Family Bank is your trusty compass. If promoted and widely adopted, the Family Bank has incredible potential to make meaningful, lasting changes in your family as well as in society. Many of the problems that plague us today, such as selfishness, greed, theft, envy, privilege, debt, and even poverty, could be greatly reduced or eliminated if more families maintained a Family Bank and continuously passed on its principles to future generations.

The Family Bank and its related functions not only promote accountability and self-reliance, but most importantly, they put time-tested systems of education, opportunity, and accountability in place to ensure their continued practice.

You're looking for answers, and I'll do my best to present what I've discovered about these quiet, successful families. This book is an attempt to reveal, explore, and broadcast the principles and practices of the Family Bank to help you start making a lasting difference in your family as quickly as possible. Thank you in advance for joining me on this journey.

2.
FORTUNE OR MISFORTUNE?

"Say not you know another entirely, till you have divided an inheritance with him."

—Johann Kaspar Lavater[4]

MOST OF US have daydreamed at one time or another about having a rich relative leave us a significant inheritance. We have probably imagined enjoying luxurious homes, vehicles, travel, and other diversions that we've always desired but for which we lacked the means. Few of us have more realistically considered how coming into money might actually injure us and destroy our closest relationships, yet that is often the result of financial windfalls.

Let me tell you a story about Ted Jones.[5] Ted owned and operated a lucrative apartment complex for several decades. As his retirement years approached, Ted wanted his children to buy him out and run the business in his stead. There was one problem: his two sons were working with him, but his two daughters were busy raising children at home.

Ted wanted to be fair with all four children but couldn't figure out how. Finally, one of Ted's sons came up with a possible solution: Ted would split ownership evenly to his four children, but the sons would repay him and the sisters for their share.

---

4   *Aphorisms on Man*, No. 157 (ca. 1788).
5   Name has been changed.

These company and inheritance "buy-outs" would occur over ten years. Everyone agreed and signed a contract with a ten-year payment schedule.

The sons worked hard in the business and kept expenses down. Most years, they funneled the majority of the profits to pay the annual "buy-out" payments to their father and sisters besides making repairs and improvements to the property. As a result, both sons were able to pay themselves only a small salary, a mere fraction of what they were paying their father and sisters each year.

About eleven years after the contract was signed, the sons were concerned about trends in the real estate market and decided to sell. They arranged for an appraisal, and the property appraised for double the value of what it was eleven years prior. An outside party purchased the business and property just before the 2008 mortgage crisis gripped the nation and property values around the country plummeted.

But another family crisis was looming. It wasn't long before the daughters discovered the business had been sold at a much higher price. They asked if their brothers would share part of the appreciated values with them, but the brothers declined. They had received little income while working ten long years and had no control over the appreciation of real estate values.

The daughters appealed to their parents unsuccessfully. They retreated in bitter outrage, accusing their brothers of manipulating their parents and accusing them all of greed and dishonesty. They stopped communicating with their brothers and parents; they also withheld their children from visiting and communicating with their brothers and parents. They stopped attending family events such as reunions, graduations, and weddings. Ted personally made multiple outreaches to each daughter to try to salvage the relationship. The daughters only responded with anger and accusations of favoritism toward the sons.

When their mother died a few years later, neither of the daughters nor any member of their families attended the funeral. Three years after that, they also declined to attend their father's funeral. A lifetime of strong family relationships had evaporated in only a few short years due to this tragic disagreement over money.

During my nearly two decades as a financial professional, I have witnessed hundreds of family disagreements about money morph into arguments, deep hatred, lawsuits, and even complete and total estrangement. Many family relationships have been strained after a relative's surplus wealth was distributed among heirs, but there are perhaps even more stories out there where debts or other financial obligations drove them apart. Disagreements over money have long been one of the top reasons for divorce, and stress from financial issues touches nearly every family negatively at some point.

> *Money is neither good nor evil; it's just a lifeless thing.*

Many who witness the estrangement of families and loved ones over money often assign blame to the money itself. I find the notion to blame money interesting because money is neither good nor evil; it's just a lifeless thing. People are responsible for their own actions, and they do crazy things with too much *and* too little money all the time. But what is it about money that makes those crazy things possible?

Think of money as a neutral "accelerant" that boosts people down the path they are already on. Wealth, and cash in particular, enables action faster and more powerfully than most resources. It tends to permit people doing good things to do even greater things, and those doing bad things feel empowered to do even worse things. Money seems to clarify and then magnify people's intentions very rapidly.

Money entrusted to those with self-discipline and a healthy

appreciation for hard work can generate remarkable prosperity. I have witnessed the children of successful entrepreneurs multiply the size and value of their parents' business ten-fold in a short amount of time. On the other hand, I have also seen people waste money to the tune of hundreds of thousands very quickly. One day, another advisor pulled me aside to show me how the eighteen-year-old grandson of his deceased client had quickly spent several hundred thousand in inheritance money. The advisor pointed to the young man's brand-new $80,000 sports car in the parking lot. "That's his third one," he said. "He crashed one and didn't like the color of the other."

We have all seen how money and relationships can make for a volatile combination, but why does that happen?

Family relationships have been the bedrock of human interaction for millennia, and we generally interact the most and are closest to our immediate family members. The conflicts and successes within a family tend to evoke stronger emotions than with other relationships. It is natural that money's amplifying power would only exacerbate family disagreements. Family members are capable of treating each other worse than strangers when a financial injustice is perceived.

It is natural that money's amplifying power would only exacerbate family disagreements.

Money seems to have an equal balance of risk and benefit potential, and the net effect depends entirely on the motives and behavior of those using it. Money can be an incredibly helpful tool when it's controlled by a trained hand. I like to compare its potential to that of fire: fire can cook our food, power our vehicles, and provide many services that are lifesaving and even luxurious. But when it is uncontrolled, fire can destroy forests, structures, and lives.

Many young people have greatly benefitted from their parents' wise financial advice and even some of their parents' financial resources at crucial crossroads. On the flip side, I have also observed family members with greater means attempt to control the behavior of other family members by financial manipulation and threats.

If money can exacerbate family problems, and it often does, then, as a neutral accelerant, it also has the equal potential to increase familial harmony. Indeed, I have observed a number of wonderfully happy families who conscientiously and systematically invested in the financial success of their children and grandchildren. They not only taught their children and grandchildren sound financial principles, but they demonstrated those principles and provided room for their family members to experiment with money and learn financial competency firsthand. Their descendants have achieved remarkable success, bringing ever-increasing joy to their parents and grandparents.

There are few things in this world that can bring greater satisfaction than working toward the financial independence and success of family members and loved ones. Yes, money can drive people apart, but with wise design, it can also bring them closer together.

> *Imagine money deepening our closest relationships.*

Imagine money deepening our closest relationships. Imagine it no longer being a topic to avoid but rather a welcome diversion in a family setting. This result is possible and probable with the right tools and actions. The secrets to this success lie in redefining roles and expectations and, most importantly, creating the right structure to provide opportunities with accountability.

3.
DILEMMA OF THE DYING

"To neglect at any time preparation for death, is to sleep on our post at a siege, but to omit it in old age, is to sleep at an attack."

—Samuel Johnson[6]

ALL LIFE ON this planet is in the business of problem-solving. Problems always arise while gathering resources such as food, water, and air; dealing with competition, predators, and disease; as well as passing on one's genes and resources to the next generation. Creatures and people who successfully navigate these problems tend to flourish.

Humans are the most successful, advanced lifeform on the planet not only because of our technology but because of the sophisticated sociality we have developed. Our willingness to assist each other gives us a tremendous advantage in our challenging world. Almost all of us grow up in families, and we usually maintain lifelong relationships with parents, siblings, children, and grandchildren that support one another and fulfill many needs. This fundamental social structure not only nourishes and sustains children within the family group, but it teaches them values and behavioral codes that lead to greater success individually and within the community. These relationships with family members tend to be the sources of our greatest disappointments and delights.

---

6   *The Rambler*, No. 78 (December 15, 1750).

Beyond our families, humans are social creatures who gather into communities for shared benefits. We share physical structures and cities and cooperate in sharing resources as equitably as possible. We set up governments to protect rights and ensure security. Some of the unique practices that tend to share resources most efficiently and benefit us while benefiting others are trade and commerce. Gathering and refining basic resources to trade has evolved over the millennia into quite complex financial systems and institutions of commerce that have led to remarkable discoveries and technological advances. To participate in those systems, most of us spend a significant portion of our lives working for money that we exchange for basic needs and luxuries alike. The pursuit and accumulation of wealth has become a nearly ubiquitous preoccupation.

Though there are many creative and inspiring ways to accumulate wealth, there is only one thing that happens to it when we die: someone else gets it. Regardless of how much or how little we have, everything is left behind to others when we are gone. Death is an inevitability for everyone irrespective of status, resources, or any desperate efforts to delay it. In a world marked by gross inequality in many respects, death is the great equalizer visiting both rich and poor alike, the famous and the forgotten. Of all the problems we encounter during our lifetime, death is a ubiquitous problem we do not have the power to solve.

There is a popular statistic that is often shared in the planning world: two out of every two people will die. While the banality of this statement makes it almost humorous, death can be a major problem for the ill-prepared. Many families, organizations, communities, and even civilizations have faced profound consequences after an individual's death. Those consequences can sometimes affect many generations that follow.

Two out of every two people will die.

As all of us will eventually succumb to death, most of us ponder the ramifications of our future departure from mortality at one time or another. This intellectual exercise triggers an inevitable series of common, self-reflective questions that I like to combine and call the "dilemma of the dying." The questions are as follows:

1. What will they say at my funeral?

It has been my experience that aged people think very introspectively as they near the end of their lives. It is natural to contemplate what positive (or negative) impact one has had on loved ones, the community, and the world, if applicable. While I have found this exercise common to the aged, it is by no means beyond the capacity of younger people as well. I would argue that those who regularly think in this way tend to be less focused on themselves and more gracious toward others. Individuals who focus on the needs of others rather than their own needs tend to live more blissfully throughout their lives.

Thankfully, most of the people I have known through my practice have passed on peacefully in this way. They nurtured personal relationships, the greatest driver of happiness in my experience, and they departed with happy feelings toward and memories of those left behind. They worked diligently in their vocations, whether in a profession or raising children in the home, and they tried to leave a lasting positive influence on those immediately around them and in their communities. Ideally, our last thoughts will be as theirs: filled with deep satisfaction and gratitude.

There are cases, however, where I have observed the problems and circumstances of the dying transferred to others at their death. My experience is that most people do not mean to leave behind a mess, but for various reasons, they avoid making certain decisions or taking actions that could clear things up for those left behind. The most obvious context where this occurs is within relationships between family members and others that involve unresolved, unkind feelings. Sometimes the damage is irreversible, but often a humble, contrite acknowledgment of the harm done is just the repayment needed to settle an emotional debt. The resulting peace is well worth it.

Other sources of problems are financial matters involving debt, tax liabilities, or other obligations that require resolution either before or after someone passes away. In most of the cases I have encountered, the size of the check that could be paid now to resolve such issues is almost always far smaller than the check that must be paid later.

> *Often, the way we will be remembered has much to do with the way we leave.*

Often, the way we will be remembered has much to do with the way we leave. The wise try to live their lives responsibly every day and in harmony with those around them, since death has the power to take any of us anytime. Less wise individuals will procrastinate or ignore pressing financial and emotional issues before dying, and their next of kin are often stuck with the bill.

2. What do I do with my stuff?

Almost everyone dies with some "stuff" in their name or possession. Whatever assets or property are listed in one's name at death are considered an "estate" from a legal and governmental standpoint. The laws regulating estates and asset transfer at death vary little from state to state. Most individuals and families, excluding some notable exceptions, end up giving most of their stuff to their next of kin. Making plans to give stuff to loved ones and charity is the essence of traditional planning today.

There are some patterns that start to emerge when you observe these kinds of cases long enough. Here is what I have noted:

- Most people have loved ones who will outlive them
- Most people would like to "help" their loved ones in their absence
- Most people would rather their "stuff" go to those loved ones than anyone else
- Most people have relationships with loved ones who unfortunately have financial or accountability issues
- Most people don't want their surviving loved ones to fight over their stuff
- Most people are likely to lose a sizable portion of their estate to taxes, debt, and other encumbrances
- Most inheritances are consumed in a brief time after they are received

Deciding what to do with one's property and possessions is sometimes depressing, since few people enjoy contemplating their mortality. The task of designating which possessions go to whom can be daunting and tedious. I have encountered a number of common attitudes toward planning in the general public that I've divided into three "camps":

1. **Ignorers:** Some choose to simply ignore or procrastinate the need to plan, and in a way, they seem to deny the reality of their eventual passing. Most in this camp find it easy to become preoccupied with other pressing issues in their businesses, investments, family, or personal health issues. The legal default of dying without a will or other post-mortem directives leaves significant uncertainty and expense for the next of kin and courts to work out. In the

ignorer's mind, any resentment or disputes that arise over their leftover assets is up to others to work out since the ignorer will not be concerned with money or property after death anyway. This *laissez-faire*, cavalier attitude toward one's wealth after death provides fertile ground for conflict, legal proceedings, and sometimes years of aggravation for those left to settle an estate.

2. **Slapdashers:** Others finally relent to outside pressure from family and advisors to plan but put together boilerplate directives with as little thinking and effort as possible. They just want to get the planning out of the way. For most attorneys, accountants, and advisors that I have observed, planning has become a transactional task that is simply "checked off." Some will update their plans occasionally as circumstances change, but most only finish their plan one time and forget about it afterward. Heirs are usually lucky to even find their deceased relatives' planning documents or remember the name of the attorney who drafted them.

   The default among slapdashers is to simply pass on wealth directly to heirs with few conditions. They usually divide their assets evenly among their children or heirs and instruct their estate's executors or trustees to distribute assets immediately or incrementally starting at their death.

   Other slapdashers elect for no assets to go to heirs in favor of charities or others. I have seen this occur in families where parents may feel that they already have entitled children and do not wish to further enable them. Those who choose this strategy effectively disinherit their heirs and place the responsibility for the management of their wealth into the hands of strangers.

3. **The Meticulous**: These are the people who try really hard to make the right plans for their wealth after they die. They take the time to contemplate the consequences of leaving or not leaving money to loved ones and institutions. In my experience, most wealthy people are in this camp, but many less wealthy people also try to properly plan for what will happen with their money. They meet regularly with their estate planning advisors and make adjustments as necessary.

   Much of their planning inevitably revolves around taxes, and the plans for assets left to heirs can become quite detailed and even capricious. For example, I have seen some plans restrict any gifts to loved ones for isolated purposes, such as education, but nothing else. Some offered to match an heir's W-2 income to try to reward hard work. Other plans set stipulations that distributions would flow only to heirs who were actively practicing a certain religion or restricted income distributions to surviving widows as long as they didn't remarry.

   The problem with these plans is they each created unintended consequences that undermined the original intent of the planning. Using the examples above, medically ill and disabled heirs received no financial assistance with their expenses from the education-only trust fund.

   The problem with most plans is they create unintended consequences.

   The heirs whose W-2s were matched worked in stressful, higher-paying jobs instead of pursuing their particular field of interest; being laid off was even more devastating than it would normally be.

Those whose benefits were dependent on their religious activity resented the requirement and ended up leaving their church anyway, and the widows of wealthy husbands ended up cohabitating with a number of boyfriends rather than remarry, contrary to the intent of the planning. The sad fact is that traditional planning in practice generally doesn't provide the right comprehensive solutions to the concerns and wishes of those who undertake it.

There is a terrible irony here associated with accumulating lots of stuff: one endures a lifetime of stress to accumulate wealth only to endure additional stress trying to decide what to do with it. Many go through the arduous process of planning and end up throwing their hands up in frustration. There seem to be too many contingencies to plan for, and it can be exhausting.

Many of these individuals reflexively designate charities as the primary recipients of their estate. But reflexive planning essentially guarantees the inevitable consumption of one's estate as well, and the surviving family can lose the potential benefits of wealth forever. Thankfully, most people are willing to make the time, effort, and expense to plan for the consequences of these types of decisions prior to their death, but they don't know the best way to do it. Few advisors do either.

3. How do I help and not hurt?

Another question comes from a familiar query one of my clients once posed: "How do we spare our children from the stress and difficulties we faced in accumulating our wealth while not making life too easy for them?" No doubt those planning to leave their wealth behind would like to promote good behavior and avoid negative outcomes, but how? Even with the help of sophisticated planning techniques to mitigate taxes and other depleting factors, and incorporating highly trained professionals to effect one's wishes, the transferred wealth tends to be wasted or worse in a short period of time.

> *Generous gifts intended to help can actually facilitate more hurt than if they hadn't been given at all.*

This creates another great irony in planning: generous gifts intended to help can actually facilitate more hurt than if they hadn't been given at all. I have witnessed hundreds of family members—from families who did extensive planning—waste the money on frivolities. Inherited wealth seems to be treated similarly to lottery winnings, where winners tend to blow the money rapidly and even declare bankruptcy within three to five years.[7] While the amounts of lottery winnings can vary significantly, the amounts winners received did not seem to make much difference. Though many winners could have easily paid off debt and created a higher, perpetual income with the money, researchers found that most winners simply consumed their winnings in a short time.[8]

What's worse, the embers of envy and unfairness are often fanned into roaring flames when litigious attorneys get involved in family squabbles that sometimes go back to childhood. Many heirs have ended up spending much of their inheritance on lawsuits against each other. I know of two sisters who sued each other over their deceased parents' estate for nearly a decade. The

---

7   https://direct.mit.edu/rest/article/93/3/961/57969/The-Ticket-to-Easy-Street-The-Financial#.VpLMM1J327Q

8   Ibid.

attorneys seemed to systematically turn much of the disputed inheritance into legal fees for themselves, and the sisters allowed bitterness and anger to consume them throughout the entire process. Lawsuits and legal settlements, including divorce, can not only quickly diminish an estate, but they can permanently destroy family relationships.

Even if heirs behave themselves, it bears repeating that research has shown that 70 percent of inherited wealth is depleted by the second generation and 90 percent by the third.[9] What a tragedy for the residue of someone's lifetime of work, one's estate, to be erased within a few short years! Add the possibility of one's wealth facilitating self-destructive behavior or lawsuits among heirs, and it is no wonder most people find estate planning unappealing.

4. What is fair?

If people wish to designate part of the estate to benefit family members and others, then a corresponding burden is deciding how much will go to whom. In my experience, few parents and grandparents are unaware of the risks involved with dumping money or assets on those unprepared to receive it; that is often the last thing they want to do. Families tend to know the strengths and weaknesses of their members, and parents usually have clear insight into their children's character and capabilities.

Fair does not necessarily mean equal.

Because every heir has varying abilities and experiences, fair does not necessarily mean equal. Dividing a considerable sum of money equally between two sons may be unwise, for example, if one of the sons has a severe gambling addiction. To avoid exacerbating that addiction, the parent(s) may choose not to

---

9 https://www.nasdaq.com/articles/generational-wealth%3A-why-do-70-of-families-lose-their-wealth-in-the-2nd-generation-2018-10

give the gambling son the same amount of money as his brother. Inevitably, the gambling son will discover the imbalance and may curse the deceased parent(s) *and* resent his brother as the more favored son. This could prompt resentment in the other brother, and he, in turn, may accuse the gambling son of ingratitude and greed, further damaging their own relationship. As most parents and benefactors desire their wealth to be used properly, determining the correct distribution among children or heirs is not intuitive.

I should repeat here that a common "solution" to the fairness issue is giving everything to someone else and, more specifically, to charity. Many who have had difficulties with certain irresponsible children often "throw the baby out with the bathwater" by giving everything to someone else. The custom among billionaires seems to be donating almost all their wealth to charity. We have seen notable figures such as Bill Gates and Warren Buffett choose this strategy not only for tax purposes but because they do not believe their children should have any more than they already have.[10]

While much good is likely to come from these charitable gifts, donated funds will eventually be consumed also. The benefactors' family members lose unparalleled opportunities for personal growth under this plan. In a way, giving one's wealth to strangers when that wealth could benefit family members and loved ones is an admission of failure.

In a way, giving one's wealth to strangers that could benefit family members and loved ones is an admission of failure.

of failure. The message to children or others who would normally

---

10   https://money.cnn.com/magazines/fortune/fortune_archive/1986/09/29/68098/index.htm

benefit from assets transferred after a loved one's death is effectively, "I don't trust you enough to leave my stuff to you. So, I'm giving it to someone else."

Obviously, parents or other benefactors would not hesitate to bequeath wealth to heirs if they knew their heirs would do good things with it. Such confidence usually comes from ensuring heirs are adequately trained and that they demonstrate their competency to manage money.

Of course, not everyone who chooses to benefit charities at death has failed to properly train their heirs to manage their money. Charitable giving is a wonderful expression of selfless generosity and benefits millions of needy recipients every year. Many estates elect to benefit both loved ones and charities for personal and tax reasons. One alternative is rarely considered, though: is it better to benefit a charity once with a large gift, or is it better to perpetually give smaller gifts that cumulatively dwarf a large gift? And what if one's heirs were the ones making the gifts from an endowment that is constantly growing? The latter is possible only with the correct planning that will be detailed in a later chapter.

4.
A TALE OF TWO BILLIONAIRES

*"Why should men leave great fortunes to their children?
If this is done from affection, is it not misguided affection?
Observation teaches that, generally speaking, it is not well for
the children that they should be so burdened.
Neither is it well for the state."*

—Andrew Carnegie[11]

SOME OF THE wealthiest families in history have implemented the creation of a "Family Bank," where they earmarked cash assets to be retained and made available through low-interest loans for the benefit and advancement of their descendants and others. Many of these families' descendants have made great fortunes and risen to prominence thanks to training and funding through their Family Banks. The continuous growth of these cash assets has also permitted these families to provide nonrepayable financial assistance to struggling family members and perpetual, annual gifts to charity. These families have extended these traditions through a legal structure made up of trusts and other entities capable of educating their younger members in matters of finance, handling the business of family banking, and funding a variety of charitable activities within and outside of the family. Thanks

---

11 Andrew Carnegie, "The Gospel of Wealth," North American Review, June 1889; https://www.carnegie.org/about/our-history/gospelofwealth/

to this planning, some Family Banks have been perpetuated for hundreds of years and provided countless financial opportunities for their members and others.

One family that has been practicing this strategy for more than seven generations, the Rockefeller family, is well-known throughout the world. In contrast to many of the Industrial Age billionaire families who consumed their wealth in a relatively brief time, Rockefeller descendants are still among the wealthiest people in the world today. What did they do differently?

John D. Rockefeller Sr. made millions refining and selling oil that led to a boom in industrial and technological innovation. When he was eighteen, his father loaned him $1,000 at 10 percent interest to help launch a produce commission, Clark and Rockefeller, which made significant profits by providing food and supplies to soldiers during the Civil War.[12] Later, the commission began investing in oil fields in Pennsylvania and the surrounding states. Rockefeller founded the Standard Oil Company in 1870 and invested millions in other sectors, such as transportation and real estate. He was a famed philanthropist whose donations to a myriad of causes totaled more than $500 million.[13] When he died in 1937, his fortune reportedly reached more than $300 billion in today's dollars, and he had successfully seized the title of "richest American" at the time, a title previously held by Cornelius Vanderbilt.[14]

When the younger John D. Rockefeller Jr. inherited his father's wealth, he quickly set about establishing trusts and other legal entities to protect and grow his family's fortune perpetually.[15]

---

12 Stewart H. Holbrook, *The Age of the Moguls* (New York: Doubleday and Company, 1953), 62.
13 https://archive.nytimes.com/www.nytimes.com/books/98/05/17/specials/rockefeller-gifts.html?module=inline
14 https://www.foxbusiness.com/markets/how-rich-is-the-rockefeller-family-today
15 https://www.cnbc.com/2018/03/26/david-rockefeller-jr-shares-4-secrets-to-wealth-and-family.html

The family emulated their patriarch's example by establishing traditions of education and training to family members to help them properly manage wealth. They have carried on John Sr.'s tradition of philanthropic dedication by donating as much as $50 million every year to charitable causes.[16] All descendants have had access to financial assistance at critical junctures in their lives. The result is that Rockefeller descendants have served as CEOs of major financial institutions, philanthropists, governors of multiple states, United States senators, and even vice president of the United States.[17] Today, the Rockefeller fortune totals less than its founder's original bequest but remains intact and growing, estimated at more than $10 billion.

Rockefeller descendants have had access to financial assistance at critical junctures in their lives.

Now let's contrast this family with another Industrial Age billionaire family, the Vanderbilts. Cornelius Vanderbilt built a transportation empire during the American Industrial Revolution that helped bring access and order to an unmapped continent. As a sixteen-year-old boy, his mother loaned him one hundred dollars[18] to purchase his first boat to ferry people and freight around New York Harbor. A shrewd and aggressive businessman, Vanderbilt soon amassed a fleet of steamships and expanded to dry land by acquiring and developing several railroad lines throughout the eastern states and westward. Vanderbilt died the wealthiest American in history; at the time, his wealth had reached $105

---

16 https://www.rockefellerfoundation.org/news/the-rockefeller-foundation-commits-50-million-in-funding-for-global-coronavirus-response-in-2020-annual-letter-covid-19-meeting-this-moment/
17 https://worldscholarshipforum.com/wealth/rockefeller-family-tree/
18 Arthur T. Vanderbilt II, Fortune's Children: The Fall of the House of Vanderbilt (New York: William Morrow, 1991), 7.

million,[19] or more than $200 billion[20] in today's dollars.

When he died, Cornelius left most of his money to his son William, to whom Cornelius famously gave this counsel prior to his death: "Any fool can make a fortune. It takes a man of brains to hold onto it after it is made."[21] William followed his father's tradition of industry by reportedly doubling the family fortune before dying eight years later.[22] But none of William's children followed their father or grandfather's example of prudence and hard work. As wealth was distributed freely to an ever-growing number of descendants, the family's fortune kept dividing and diminishing. Heirs consumed their wealth conspicuously, and the Vanderbilt name became synonymous with decadent living. For example, heirs were known to host lavish parties at their ten spectacular residences on Manhattan Island and other château-like properties, such as the Biltmore in North Carolina and the Breakers in Rhode Island.[23]

> "Inherited wealth is a real handicap to happiness."

Though they lived a life of unparalleled privilege, some of the Vanderbilts experienced dissatisfaction in their opulent lifestyles. Cornelius Vanderbilt's grandson William Vanderbilt II once remarked, "My life was never destined to be quite happy. It was laid out along lines which I could not foresee, almost from earliest childhood. It has left me with nothing to hope for, with nothing definite to seek or strive

---

19   Vanderbilt, 49.
20   https://www.businessinsider.com/how-vanderbilt-dynasty-lost-its-fortune-2017-12
21   https://www.forbes.com/sites/natalierobehmed/2014/07/14/the-vanderbilts-how-american-royalty-lost-their-crown-jewels/?sh=5fea7248353b
22   https://www.businessinsider.com/how-vanderbilt-dynasty-lost-its-fortune-2017-12
23   Ibid.

for. Inherited wealth is a real handicap to happiness."[24]

When 120 Vanderbilt descendants met together at Vanderbilt University for a family reunion in 1973, there wasn't a single millionaire among them.[25] By the time fifth-generation Vanderbilt and *CNN* anchor Anderson Cooper was born, he confirmed there was no "pot of gold" waiting for him either.[26] Cooper started his career independently working as a young freelance reporter and went so far as to forge press credentials to land a breakthrough scoop in Burma/Myanmar.[27] Because the Vanderbilt family had divided their remaining wealth at each successive generation with little or no direction for how it was to be managed, their remarkable wealth rivaling any in history was lost forever. While there have been many wealthy millionaires and billionaires throughout history, only a few of their families have been able to retain and grow their wealth beyond a few decades.

> "There wasn't a single millionaire among them.."

Why is generational wealth so quickly and easily consumed? Generational wealth is susceptible to two kinds of threats: external and internal. External threats include income taxes, capital gains taxes, estate taxes, claims by creditors for unpaid debts, and lawsuits by business interests, the Internal Revenue Service, and even strangers. Internal threats can materialize from wasteful or contentious heirs, and many plans try to set limiting provisions to avoid benefitting spendthrift, self-destructive, or litigious heirs.

Traditional estate planning tries to protect wealth from consumption and exploitation by putting up legal barriers against

---

24 *New York Herald*, July 23, 1920, quoted in Vanderbilt, 356.
25 Vanderbilt, 7–8.
26 https://www.foxbusiness.com/business-leaders/gloria-vanderbilt-anderson-cooper-inheritance-report
27 https://web.archive.org/web/20070703033851/http://www.mediabistro.com/articles/cache/a1582.asp

these external and internal threats. In practice, traditional planning does a lousy job fulfilling people's wishes and avoiding the external and internal threats to most estates. While external threats tend to remove a sizable portion of the estate, the unscrupulous behavior of spendthrift heirs often dissipates whatever is left of it. As mentioned, research has shown that 70 percent of inherited wealth is depleted by the second generation and 90 percent by the third.[28] That statistic ostensibly includes the estates of most wealthy people who did extensive planning with a team of financial professionals.

So, what do the minority of families do differently to successfully preserve their wealth?

The Rockefellers and others made a commitment to their family members' future opportunities, not outcomes. They provided their descendants with the financial means to pursue their dreams without entitling them. Most critically, they didn't follow the traditional planning model of doling out inheritances; instead, they set up a Family Bank that could lend out family money at low interest for worthy endeavors. "Board members" of the Family Bank provided educational training to family members and others in finance and management. To perpetuate their banks through subsequent generations, they established legal entities holding cash-equivalent assets that were protected, grown, and used to provide financial assistance to family members and others. Most importantly, these banks hold the ideal legacy assets that provide funding for family members' financial activities and investments that can ensure their perpetuity. We will explore these practices in greater detail in the coming chapters.

---

28   https://www.nasdaq.com/articles/generational-wealth%3A-why-do-70-of-families-lose-their-wealth-in-the-2nd-generation-2018-10

5.
WHO ELSE KNOWS ABOUT THIS?

"It is one thing to show a man that he is in error, and another to put him in possession of the truth."

—John Locke[29]

THROUGHOUT MY CAREER, I've witnessed thousands of thoughtful parents, grandparents, and other relatives seek to benefit their families and communities with their wealth and wisdom. Many have tried to teach and financially assist members of their families and others during their lifetimes with mixed results. Others have postponed any financial arrangements until after their death, and they sought to solve any potential family money issues through extensive planning. Their attorneys and other advisors recommended the use of wills, trusts, and other entities to prevent heirs from wasting their inheritance or using it for ill.

Many of these long-term plans sought to transfer wealth gradually or through "incentives" rather than through gifts. For example, some plans metered out funds or assets to heirs as annual income instead of distributing large sums. Others set up income benchmarks that would trigger matching cash gifts. Despite their creativity and complexity, these attempts just delayed the inevitable: wealth was eventually distributed and

---

29 *An Essay Concerning Human Understanding*, Book 4, Chapter 7, Section 2, 1690.

consumed, and the risk of self-indulgence never disappeared. Lawsuits between heirs sometimes followed. I have witnessed too many relationships and successful businesses destroyed by financial conflicts.

> *Most of the plans I have seen create unintended consequences that would cause the deceased to roll over in their graves.*

Most of the plans I've seen have resulted in unintended consequences that would cause the deceased parents or grandparents to roll over in their graves. These planning techniques all attempted to avoid the same inevitable problems that nearly every family seems to experience, but they lacked the proper tools and processes to prevent them. And very few family members were even aware of these plans, much less fully committed to making them work in the long-term.

I have been especially chagrined to hear of loved ones and acquaintances dealing with major disagreements and lawsuits related to gifts, loans, and distributions of family money through inheritances. I have seen too many close relationships become strained or destroyed by misunderstandings about money. Most disputes arose when individuals and families made financial arrangements improperly or inadequately, and I have only identified very few who have done it right. The pitfalls of inadequate or even comprehensive traditional planning can permanently damage even the closest relationships.

A few years ago, I discovered the Family Bank concept that has changed my thinking and my life's work forever. In the fall of 2018, an estate planning attorney requested a visit from an agent of one of the companies I represented, and it was forwarded to me.

I had never met the attorney, but I was happy to respond to his request and meet him in person. After exchanging pleasantries, the attorney declared, "I'm setting up a Family Bank and I need your help to fund it."

At the time, I had never heard of a Family Bank and asked him what he meant by it. He said he had recently been introduced to an ingenious way he could set up a personal cash reserve for emergencies and investments, properly train his children in financial matters, and provide a means for generations of his descendants to enjoy the benefits of wealth without the customary risks of entitlement, selfishness, or other common problems triggered by inherited wealth. He explained the idea so simply and persuasively, I was intrigued. That set my research of this concept in motion.

Over the next few years, I talked to almost everyone I could about the Family Bank as described by the attorney. I searched libraries, bookstores, and the internet for more information, but I found very little on the topic. With the exception of only a handful of websites, articles, and a few books I've identified at the time of this writing, there is very little in print about it. The books that do mention it discuss only *part* of the idea, and they fail to articulate all the basic principles and essential practices required to run and perpetuate successful Family Banks. It reminded me of the ancient parable of the "Blind Men and the Elephant," where each man was convinced of the elephant's entire anatomy based on his respective handhold (a trunk, a tail, and so on). The handful of books I was able to find on the topic also ended up emphasizing the same things every time: education and values. Every book felt like the same read, just with different stories.

Don't get me wrong; I love education and good values. But many of us are interested in implementing practical means to pass on those values, not just itemizing and celebrating the values themselves. The few books that mention the Family Bank usually do so in passing, and each author seems to accept a long-held tradition that has facilitated heirs' poor behavior and the eventual consumption of family wealth: gifting. The consensus message seems to be, "Just make lots of rules and compel your family to follow them." The insight of the estate attorney in 2018 was clear: avoid gifting (with certain exceptions) in favor of low-interest loans. This will promote accountability and productivity.

The beauty and simplicity of this concept is readily discernable to all.

I knew much smarter people had pondered these issues extensively and that there must be some successful practices I could easily discover and share. Seeking some examples, I consulted with other professionals and advisors with far more education and experience, but they were wholly unfamiliar with the concept of the Family Bank. I met in person with the senior partners of some of the largest law and accounting firms in multiple states, as well as dozens of highly successful and experienced financial and estate planners, but few of them had heard of the Family Bank. But my discoveries always made sense to them, and the beauty and simplicity of the concept is readily discernible to all.

For the past few years, I have been continuously perplexed as to why more people haven't heard about the Family Bank or adopted it as a model in their thinking and planning. With limited information, I couldn't point any of my clients or others to an authoritative source for reference. Because my clients asked so many follow-up questions, and because I had insufficient information on the subject, I had to work out most of those answers on my own through research and professional experience.

The next time you visit with an attorney or a financial professional, you might try asking if he or she has even heard the term "Family Bank." If so, press for details. Chances are, he or she won't have much to tell you. Family Banks are extremely uncommon, but this is a trend we must reverse. They are a remarkable, simple solution to a number of complex problems and concerns that people and society encounter regarding wealth and family.

6.

THE PROBLEM WITH MOST PLANNING

"He does not possess wealth; it possesses him."

—Benjamin Franklin[30]

I RECENTLY WATCHED a movie called *Knives Out* that amusingly captures some of the problems that occur in families when it comes to planning. If you have not yet seen it and cannot stand movie spoilers, I recommend you put this book down and go watch it before reading on.

Now that you have seen it or do not mind reading some spoilers, I would like to cite a critical scene in the movie where the plot takes a dramatic turn. With great trepidation and expectation, the family awaits a reading aloud of the deceased's recently updated will. The details of this document were kept secret while he was alive, to be revealed to his family members in person only after his death.

All the assembled relatives smile and hold their spouses' hands tightly in hopes that they will receive part of his substantial wealth. To the shock of all, the will's instructions direct all of the deceased's assets to be conferred upon the deceased's nurse. The family members gasp and look at each other in disbelief as they realize they have all been disinherited. After a few seconds of tense

---

30   *Poor Richard's Almanack,* May 1734.

silence, the oldest son stands up and says something like, "Uh . . . no. That's not. That's . . . no. That can't be. Can I see that, please?"³¹

The family begins talking among themselves, their voices slowly rising in frustration and anger. Accusations fly against the nurse, and she, in turn, attempts to make a hasty exit. The family follows her out and surrounds her car as they try to plead their case. Through the course of the film, family members predictably attempt to cajole, manipulate, intimidate, and even kill the nurse when things don't go their way. She ends up keeping the inherited assets and acts virtuously in contrast to the family members' mostly despicable behavior.

While watching the film, I found myself asking a number of questions:

- Why do the family members become so nasty once they learn they've lost their inheritance?
- Why does "losing" money that was never theirs have such an effect on people?
- Why was their terrible (and comical) reaction actually predictable?
- Where did the tradition to give family members an inheritance come from, anyway?

The deceased family members' behavior (or, more aptly, misbehavior) is not only due to their questionable motives and character but to a critical flaw in the planning world regarding family finances: they believed they should be benefitted by their deceased father and grandfather at his death. They were his "heirs," and heirs typically receive their deceased relatives' money or property precisely because of their genetic or legal

---

31 *Knives Out*. Dir. Rian Johnson. Lionsgate Entertainment, 2019. Film.

relationship to him. Though this expectation was presumptuous, it wasn't really their fault: that is the default practice in traditional planning, and lamentably scenes like this are not uncommon.

> *Entitlement often connotes receiving something for nothing.*

What is an "heir," anyway? The classic definition is someone legally entitled to property or other valuable things (like a rank or title) at someone's death. Note that word *entitled*, and you see where the trouble can begin in a financial context. Entitlement often connotes receiving something for nothing.

Most heirs have a biological connection to the deceased through a family relationship. And how do heirs typically become entitled? They simply luck out by being born into the right family. Warren Buffett calls this phenomenon winning "the ovarian lottery."[32]

We have all seen spoiled heirs of wealthy families engage in disgraceful and self-destructive behavior. Their misdeeds are widely broadcast (and even celebrated by some) in the media. Receiving a family inheritance wasn't always so dangerous. In fact, several hundred years ago, legally entitling heirs with property or other things at death was proper and preferable.

Before the Industrial Revolution, around 80 percent of American citizens lived and worked on farms.[33] A family's sustenance came from their own land and animals, and any surplus was traded or sold for additional necessities or wants. The most valuable asset that a family owned was commonly the farmland itself. Since few had the financial resources to purchase farmland with currency or credit, it remained an illiquid asset

---

32 As quoted in Alice Schroeder, The Snowball: Warren Buffett and the Business of Life (New York: Random House, 2008).
33 https://www.nber.org/system/files/chapters/c1567/c1567.pdf

passed on from generation to generation.

Passing on farmland was the opposite of an entitlement; it provided an opportunity and a living to those willing to maintain the farm, as was the case in the majority of families. Though land ownership was technically a gift to the next generation, that gift required effort and intelligence if those who inherited it were to realize value from the farm's resources.

What has changed since then? The numbers have completely reversed. In 2019, nearly 80 percent of employed Americans work in the "services" industry, and only 1.3 percent work on farms.[34] Today's estates are far larger and have much more complicated assets than the farms of two centuries ago. The average estate in 2019 was $305,200 for noncollege-educated parents[35] and $1,519,900 for college-educated parents. The largest asset in most estates is still property (the family home), but it is only rarely connected to a farm. After the family home, retirement accounts, stocks and bonds, vehicles, and other assets, most of which did not even exist two hundred years ago, now comprise the lion's share of a family's estate.

Another substantial change in estates today as compared to those of two hundred years ago is taxes. The Progressive era brought about several types of taxes that directly affect estate planning. In 1913, the sixteenth amendment was ratified, permitting the federal government and states to collect income taxes. Most estates today have some type of deferred tax accounts like IRAs or annuities where the deceased's beneficiaries pay tax through their individual income tax brackets.

Congress also passed the Revenue Act of 1916, creating the modern estate tax and taxing the transfer of wealth above certain amounts from deceased individuals to their heirs. The exemption

---

34   https://www.bls.gov/emp/tables/employment-by-major-industry-sector.htm
35   https://www.federalreserve.gov/publications/files/scf20.pdf p.11

amounts and percentages have fluctuated greatly since then, but typically only very large estates have to worry about this one.

Because today's estates are dramatically larger and more asset-diverse than those of two hundred years ago, the traditional approach to estate planning is woefully out of date. Society has become much more connected through innovations in communication and transportation, and those breakthroughs have facilitated greater wealth and market accessibility. Most assets, even those considered less liquid, like real estate, can be exchanged relatively easily for cash in a short amount of time. We are living in the age of eBay, but most people are doing estate planning like we're still living in the colonies.

> *We are living in the age of eBay while most people are planning like we're still living in the colonies.*

Family disputes over inheritance could be almost comical if only they weren't so destructive to relationships and the estate itself. The traditional planning practice of gifting money or assets to people can sometimes result in the exact opposite than what was intended. Unfortunately, much of the planning being done today is not likely to prevent these outcomes because it is fundamentally flawed.

7.

WHAT PLANNERS GET WRONG

"The more laws and orders are made prominent, the more thieves and bandits there will be."

—Lao Tzu[36]

"ALL RIGHT, HOW much do you want the little rascals to get?"

One prominent, experienced attorney, who has helped many of our clients, regularly poses this exact question during his first visit with new clients. After making customary introductions and briefly discussing the basics of estate planning, he uses this question to try to get to what he views as the bottom line of traditional planning in a lighthearted way.

Traditional planning typically begins with the help of "estate planners," such as attorneys, tax accountants, and financial professionals. Because there are often tax, legal, business, and family issues to address, each member of the team has a different role: attorneys draft the necessary legal documents to meet the person's wishes and needs, tax accountants assist with business and tax reporting, and financial professionals or advisors encourage clients to act and direct the coordination of the team. They also assist with the purchase of life insurance or other financial products to "fund" clients' wishes and provide liquidity to the estate. It is common for all these professionals to work concertedly on an estate case.

---

36 *Tao-te Ching*, Chapter 57, Wing-Tsit Chan, trans.

People who elect to go through the planning process primarily have their families and loved ones in mind. Yet many estate planners are trained to focus on the legal and financial elements of planning while concerns for relationships and family legacy issues take a back seat. As a result, the process can become very transactional.

In the minds of nearly all the estate planners I've met, the crux of traditional planning lies in arbitrarily designating amounts to the three different places they believe money or assets can exclusively go after death:

1. other individuals or legal entities, which includes family members and friends,

2. charity, a common beneficiary for many estates, and

3. the Internal Revenue Service for taxable assets, especially very large estates subject to the estate tax that we'll examine later.

One of the quickest ways to deduce the respective percentages according to the traditional planning model is to ask clients how much inheritance they want their children or loved ones to receive.

Determining the amount of any inheritance is an effective time-saver with traditional planning. For example, if a client wishes to give all her money to charity, the planning will take a different direction than if she wants most to go to her family. Sometimes a tax liability can be offset by planned charitable donations, paid by the proceeds of life insurance, or both.

Because most estate planners are trained to focus on mitigating the external and internal threats of taxes, creditors, lawsuits, divorce, and spendthrift or litigious heirs, the personal opportunities and development of their clients' descendants isn't usually the expressed purpose of their work. Trust documents, for example, generally do not read like family "mission statements." Rather, they have all the charm of verbose legal contracts. Many planners have little idea of what their clients would like to see happen in their families, and they effectively ignore the purpose and implications of gifting substantial amounts of wealth to heirs in the first place. I am not sure I have ever heard a planner question the reasoning behind a client's wish to gift a large amount of money or assets to an heir, regardless of the circumstances. Perhaps these planners may view their job as doing whatever their clients want, and they may feel uncomfortable questioning a practice as common as gifting.

> *Planning documents have all the charm of verbose legal contracts.*

A few years ago, I received a customary email from an insurance brokerage firm celebrating a recently completed case. The firm was delighted to report that one of their agents had helped a retired female client successfully convert a large amount of cash into an even larger insurance benefit she intended to leave equally to her two adult daughters. The headline of the email read, "Agent Helps Client Turn One Million into Three Million, Tax-Free!" While growing money for clients is laudable through insurance or investments, I found myself wondering if the agent was really helping the client and her family by facilitating large gift giving.

I wondered:

- What was the client trying to accomplish by the gift?
- Was each daughter equally capable of managing and

growing such a generous sum of money?

- Had the client considered the risks of leaving substantial amounts of cash to her daughters?

- Did the client have any hope that the money could help her daughters in specific ways, and had she made the necessary plans to ensure her wishes were respected?

- Did those plans have "guardrails" to protect the cash from being wasted, especially if the daughters needed to be protected from themselves?

Many attorneys and other advisors would respond to these questions by saying that they know exactly how to solve these client concerns: clients just need to add a number of provisions and clauses to their planning documents that strictly direct the distribution of their wealth. These provisions fall into two categories: method and rules.

METHOD

"Sprinkling" is the same as "dumping," just more slowly.

Because spendthrift heirs are notorious at blowing large sums of money, and because a windfall of money can sometimes facilitate vices and addictions, many believe that a more incremental method of gifting can avoid these problems. Specifically, many attorneys and advisors recommend the popular practice of spacing out the timing and amount of gifts by "sprinkling" instead of making "lump-sum" gifts. Sprinkling wealth more gradually on heirs may be done specifically to avoid the risky outcomes of lump-sum gifting, but it is essentially the same as "dumping," just doing it more slowly.

With sprinkling, heirs still receive wealth by virtue of their relationship to the giver, not necessarily for any developmental purpose linked with accountability. Sprinkling may delay the gift's consumption, but it may not prevent it. In my experience, the heirs I've seen who received sprinkled gifts have tended to consume or waste the gift regardless of the amount. The potential for heirs suing each other or wasting any wealth they receive still remains, whether the wealth is received quickly or slowly.

RULES

Remember how the consensus message in the planning community seems to be, "Just make lots of rules for your money and compel your family to follow them"? Many attorneys and advisors suggest the further step of articulating strict stipulations for the heirs' proper use of their clients' wealth. Many attorneys add *no-contest* and *spendthrift* clauses to wills and trusts, for example, to prevent the outcomes that clients fear most, such as family infighting and wasteful consumption.

> *"Just make lots of rules for your money and compel your family to follow them."*

While fastidious restrictions may seem effective on paper, many heirs regularly challenge these (and other restrictions placed on them). Indeed, it seems to be human nature to bristle at rules governing the use of what we may view as our property or birthright and to seek ways around them. Heirs have been known to dispute the legitimacy of a will, for example, if a wealth distribution is not in their favor. Disgruntled heirs have suggested that their deceased loved one was inappropriately pressured or displayed symptoms of mental decline when the will was drafted; with these claims, the will may be invalided by a court. Finally, once assets are distributed to heirs, the deceased's executor or trustee may not be able to prevent the wasteful consumption of distributed assets unless there is constant oversight of the heirs' activities. Ensuring heirs' compliance with trust provisions can be burdensome, uncomfortable, and maybe even impossible for trustees.

Those who believe in no direct distributions to heirs in favor of strategies *for the benefit* of heirs can likewise have their intentions undermined. A trustee whose responsibilities include assisting heirs in purchasing a home, for example, may make payments directly to a title or mortgage company instead of to the family member. However, heirs may recoup the gifted payments by potentially selling the property anytime since the property is likely in their name. Thus, heirs may ultimately take possession of the wealth whenever they want with a bit of a work-around.

Most attorneys and advisors seem to put clients through multiple rounds of "Whac-A-Mole."

Because clients may not be able to foresee every possible contingency, the best detailed plans tend not to accomplish their objectives. Many attorneys and advisors seem to put clients through multiple rounds of planning "Whac-A-Mole," trying to cover a cascade of possible outcomes with plans to prevent or mitigate every future problem. This type of reactive planning may remind people of prescription drug treatments, where certain medications may be prescribed for the side effects of other medications and more for the side effects of those medications. All this effort to prevent entitlement, eliminate wasteful consumption, and protect heirs from themselves may, in fact, defeat the purpose of planning; heirs may end up resenting their deceased relatives for putting restrictions on the gifts they receive or believe they should receive, and givers would regret sharing any gifts in the first place if they knew their relatives were resentful.

Families shouldn't have to centrally plan their family members' financial activities. "Negative" or "reactive" planning tends to be an uncomfortable exercise because it's not natural. Indeed, since most believe freedom and opportunity are fundamental to the human condition (and crucial for economic success), families should embrace the principles of liberty and agency in regard to their wealth planning. Rather than prescribing a panoply of rules that can hamper individual free will and personal growth, proper care should be taken to promote family members' independence to facilitate greater personal development and success.

The Family Bank's broad guidelines replace detailed edicts, and family members can be held responsible for the outcome of their own choices rather than being restrained from making specific choices in the first place. These choices will center around activities with wealth potential such as education, investments, property ownership, and business creation, allowing family members to exercise significant creativity in these activities. The Family Bank doesn't have to govern its members; members *govern themselves* through access to the proper training and tools.

> The Family Bank doesn't have to govern its members; members govern themselves.

Opportunities and incentives are more powerful than threats and coercion. The Family Bank embodies these truths, and it accomplishes its mission by providing the right assistance at the right time and in the right way. Family members enjoy greater self-confidence and prosperity through their own efforts, not by any birthright. What a relief for families *not* to feel obligated to plan the future of their family members top-down!

So, why don't more estate planners recommend creating a Family Bank? I once asked an experienced attorney familiar with the Family Bank this very question, and he replied that such a lack is through unfamiliarity with the Family Bank or through laziness. Unfortunately, most attorneys and advisors plan the exact same way, and any shift in thinking or professional practice would likely take greater effort than what they typically provide in their basic services.

Most estate planners may not realize that even though the Family Bank is technically part of the first destination for wealth per federal and state gifting rules, family, it essentially operates as a fourth option since no one person takes ownership or full control of the assets within the bank. The Family Bank can provide funding for the other two wealth destinations (charity and the Internal Revenue Service) as well, with the capacity to pay any applicable taxes and make charitable donations. In that way, estate planners can still fulfill their fiduciary and legal responsibility by adequately addressing their clients' tax and legal liabilities while bypassing all the disadvantages inherent in traditional planning, such as entitlement, wasteful consumption, and others previously mentioned.

The estate planning attorney quoted at the beginning of this chapter is proficient and experienced, but his initial question—"How much do you want the little rascals to get?"—reveals a flawed premise. Indeed, planning shouldn't have to center around gifting. Even with strong, articulated expectations and rules, gifting more often than not results in unintended consequences. The attorney's first questions with clients should be "What do you want to see happen with your money?" and "What would you like to see happen in your family?" Pondering these questions more thoroughly and considering the actual consequences of traditional planning would lead him and other planners to rightly conclude that default planning practices are often inadequate at accomplishing their clients' goals. When the same practices most attorneys employ repeatedly fail to produce desired outcomes, planners have a professional obligation to get back to the drawing board.

8
THE BORROWER'S CLUB

"Life is real! Life is earnest!
And the grave is not its goal;
Dust thou art, to dust returnest,
Was not spoken of the soul."

—Henry Wadsworth Longfellow[37]

"HAVE YOU EVER seen a hearse pulling a U-Haul trailer?" That question caused me to pause for a second and then smile at its comedic absurdity. The client smiled as well. The estate planner I was observing had distilled the complexity of end-of-life financial decisions into a simple fact: when we die, our wealth and possessions stay here. No matter how hard we try to hang onto them, they cannot go with us. Someone else will take possession of them.

> *"Have you ever seen a hearse pulling a U-Haul trailer?"*

There are notable examples of those who tried to hang on to their wealth anyway. Ancient pharaohs in Egypt believed entombing themselves in magnificent pyramids with their priceless treasures would permit those goods to pass with them into the next world. Similarly, the Chinese emperor Qin Shi Huang commissioned artists to carve thousands of terracotta warriors,

---

37 "A Psalm of Life," St. 1–2 (1838).

horses, diplomats, musicians, and even acrobats to accompany him in the afterlife. We know that these efforts failed, of course, because those treasures are still here for the rest of us to enjoy.

A fact of mortality is that regardless of who we are and what we do, none of us truly *own* anything beyond our lifetime. The temporary ownership of our possessions is immediately and permanently severed at death, and all the resources we've accumulated will remain here on earth. Everything we have created, enjoyed, or abused will eventually be left to someone or something else. Those resources are endlessly recycled generation after generation in a remarkably stable system that supports all manner of life. In fact, all the materials that make up and support our lives have already been here for billions of years. The same water molecules we drink today were drunk by the dinosaurs. And everything we have and *think* we own doesn't really belong to us; just ask the dinosaurs.

Because ownership is temporary and all resources will inevitably be forfeited after our lifetime, *owning* resources is actually *borrowing* resources. Our possessions, our resources, our physical body, and even the time in which we live and act are all part of a system in which we participate as *borrowers*, and not one of us has any permanent control or ownership over that system.

> *Owning resources is actually borrowing resources.*

Each generation of humans effectively makes up a "borrower's club" including people who use resources while sojourning in mortality and subsequently cede everything to the next generation. Forces on this planet well beyond our ability to control will quickly erase our footprints, just as civilization after civilization of humans have gone through the same cycle for thousands of years. And all the material that makes up the matter here will still be here in one form or another when thousands of generations following this one are long gone. The comedian George Carlin once summed up our experience on earth this way:

> Compared to people, the planet is doing great. Been here four and a half billion years. . . . The planet has been through a lot worse than us. Been through all kinds of things worse than us: been through earthquakes, volcanoes, plate tectonics, continental drifts, solar flares, sunspots, magnetic storms, the magnetic reversal of the poles, hundreds of thousands of years of bombardment by comets and asteroids and meteors, worldwide floods, tidal waves, worldwide fires, erosion, cosmic rays, recurring ice ages, and we think some plastic bags and aluminum cans are going to make a difference?
>
> The planet isn't going anywhere, we are! We're going away and we won't leave much of a trace either . . . maybe a little styrofoam . . . maybe . . . little styrofoam. The planet will be here, we'll be long gone; just another failed mutation; just another closed-end biological mistake; an evolutionary cul-de-sac. The planet will shake us off like a bad case of fleas, a surface nuisance.[38]

> *Borrowing implies an additional responsibility, one that is often described as a "stewardship."*

Though our influence may be limited by scope and time, we humans can have a substantial effect on our immediate surroundings and particularly on the next generation. Borrowing with this generation-spanning power implies an additional responsibility, one that is often described as a "stewardship."

---

38 https://scrapsfromtheloft.com/2019/08/22/george-carlin-saving-planet-transcript/

Compared to other life forms on the planet, our intelligence and technology have given us the ability to manipulate resources to suit our needs and wants unlike any other creature.

While elephants can clear paths in the jungle and beavers can dam streams, humans have cut down entire forests and permanently altered the course of major rivers. Our access to natural resources is privileged, and the wise use of natural resources can permit greater health, enjoyment, and increased populations of humans on the planet. Alternatively, the misuse of those resources can negatively affect natural environments and bring increased disease and death to humans and ecosystems alike. Though the duration of our lifetime is extremely short compared to the earth's four-billion-year history, what we do today can have a powerful effect on the kind of world our children inherit.

There is a dichotomy of rights and responsibilities that characterizes most borrowing agreements. *Rights* in this context can be defined as possession, privileges, and powers. *Responsibilities* relate to the proper discharge of those privileges and powers with accountability to others. A common example of borrowing that displays these characteristics is that of a home mortgage. The borrower receives physical possession of the home with the right to use it, make changes to it, sell it, and realize gain or loss as a result of the sale.

The relationship between rights and responsibility can explain both good and bad behavior.

The borrower simultaneously takes on the responsibility to pay the monthly mortgage payment, applicable home insurance premiums, and property taxes, among other things. The borrower is ultimately responsible for repaying the full mortgage value with interest on a set repayment schedule.

This relationship between rights and responsibility can explain the good behavior of some and the exploitative behavior of others. A mental exercise I like to do with clients is to explore this relationship on a pad of paper. I draw a big box and divide it evenly with an X and Y axis intersecting in the middle. On the top of the box, I write *More Responsibilities*, and at the bottom of the box, I write *No Responsibilities*. On the right side of the box, I write *More Rights*, and on the left side of the box, I write *No Rights*. Here's how it looks:

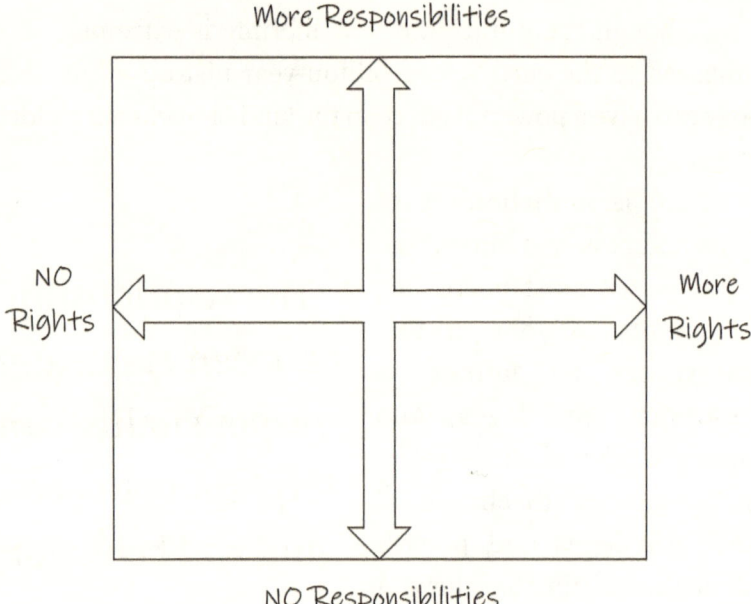

My next task is to label the different quadrants that correspond with the different amounts of rights and responsibilities, respectively. Moving counterclockwise from the top left quadrant, I first discuss the status of one who has many obligations but no rights or privileges. That is more or less the definition of slavery, and I write Servitude in the northwest quadrant. Someone with no rights and no responsibility is effectively excluded from any part of the system, so I write Exclusion in the southwest quadrant. Those with many rights and privileges but little or no accountability can be described as entitled, and that's what I write in the southeast quadrant. Entitled is a term that almost everyone knows and understands well, and it's often a feared outcome and primary concern of those doing planning. Finally, in the northeast quadrant, I write Stewardship, which is the term correlated with simultaneously increased responsibility and rights. Here's how the fully labeled diagram looks:

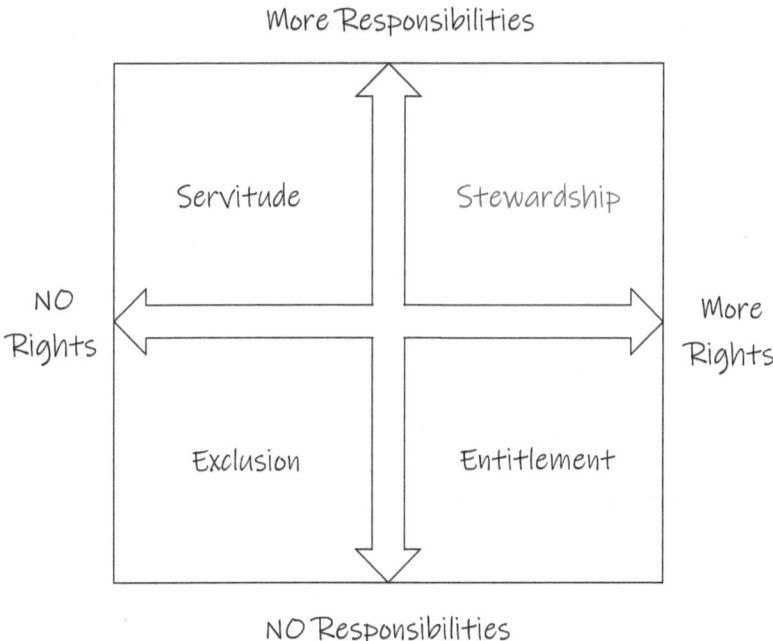

Estate attorney and author David York described the relationship between rights and responsibilities this way: "Entitlement comes when we focus only on our rights without taking into account any corresponding responsibilities. Enslavement, on the other hand, is when we have only responsibilities and no rights. Living an entrusted life happens when we balance both our rights and our responsibilities."39

Stewardship is the simultaneous exercise of privileges and responsibility as a part of a greater purpose or design. Historically, stewards were entrusted with riches or resources by their master or lord and charged to accomplish a specific task. In order to fulfill their duty, stewards received powers or rights directly from their lord that typically permitted them to conduct business on his behalf as his duly appointed representatives. The powers, rights, or privileges that were bestowed upon a steward were designed for a specific purpose and often for a temporary time. Stewards also had the responsibility to report their activities to their lord. They were held accountable for the proper or improper discharge of their duty, and they received a reward or punishment accordingly. Stewardship is therefore a perfect blend of accountability and opportunity for one seeking to grow and prove himself or herself to a loved one or higher power.

> *Stewardship is a perfect blend of accountability and opportunity.*

What are the marks of stewardship? Stewards recognize that they have temporary ownership of entrusted resources that are not their own. They not only treat their lord's resources well, but they are grateful for the opportunity to manage them. These resources are not wasted on self-indulgent activities; rather, they are invested with care and constant supervision. Stewards know that they may be required to return the entrusted resources in the future, and their stewardship requires them to multiply the resource productively.

Stewardship also implies that one will eventually be held accountable for the proper use of an entrusted resource. Historically, stewards regularly communicated the status of

---

39 Unpublished email received on 6/30/21; modified with permission.

their stewardship with their lord or master, and they took care to manage their entrusted resources according to their lord's wishes. That accounting may occur individually with us today as a deathbed reflection. Many believe it will occur with deity after this life. At a minimum, our children will hold us accountable for anything we do with our entrusted resources that directly influences their future happiness and opportunities.

Finally, stewardship can lead to a future reward or punishment. Stewards who follow their lord's instructions may not only retain their positions but may enjoy even greater rights and responsibilities. Those who disregard the charge can expect to lose those delegated rights and responsibilities. Perhaps the greatest reward to humankind's proper discharge of its stewardship is a happy and successful progeny.

Some may consider the impermanence of ownership and the principles of borrowing and stewardship to be analogous to those of collectivism. That couldn't be further from the truth. Stewardship is not the denial of private ownership; rather, the physical possession, control, and consequences associated with private ownership are critical for stewards to fulfill their responsibilities. The principles of stewardship not only guide the proper administration of property and resources to benefit oneself, but, by extension, they benefit others as well.

The control and consequences of private ownership are critical for stewardship.

One of the classic historical events that demonstrates this fact occurred when Puritan refugees fled their native England aboard the Mayflower in 1620 for religious freedom and greater opportunity on this continent. To fund their venture and equalize the distribution of lands and resources, the emigrants all entered into a partnership agreement where, "For seven years there was to be no individual property or trade, but the labor of the colony was to be organized according to the different capacities of the settlers."[40] William Bradford, governor of the fledgling Plymouth Colony, recorded the dismal results of this arrangement in his personal diary:

> The failure of this experiment of communal service, which was tried for several years, and by good and honest men proves the emptiness of the theory of Plato and other ancients, applauded by some of later times, —that the taking away of private property, and the possession of it in community, by a commonwealth, would make a state happy and flourishing; as if they were wiser than God. For in this instance, community of property (so far as it went) was found to breed much confusion and discontent, and retard much employment which would have been to the general benefit and comfort. For the young men who were most able and fit for service objected to being forced to spend their time and strength in working for other men's wives and children, without any recompense. The strong man or the resourceful man had no more share of food, clothes, etc., than the weak man who was not able to do a quarter the other could. This was thought injustice. The aged and graver men, who were ranked and equalized in labour, food, clothes, etc., with the humbler and younger ones, thought it some indignity and disrespect to them. As for men's wives who were obliged to do service for other men, such as cooking, washing their clothes, etc., they considered it a kind of slavery, and many husbands would not brook it. This feature of it would have been worse

---

40   John Andrew Doyle, *English Colonies in America, Volume 2: The Puritan Colonies* (1889), 42.

still, if they had been men of an inferior class. If (it was thought) all were to share alike, and all were to do alike, then all were on an equality throughout, and one was as good as another; and so, if it did not actually abolish those very relations which God himself has set among men, it did at least greatly diminish the mutual respect that is so important should be preserved amongst them. Let none argue that this is due to human failing, rather than to this communistic plan of life in itself. I answer, seeing that all men have this failing in them, that God in His wisdom saw that another plan of life was fitter for them.[41]

After two years of scant harvests and feuding among the colonists, Bradford recorded the solution that ultimately saved this company of settlers:

> At length after much debate, the Governor, with the advice of the chief among them, allowed each man to plant corn for his own household, and to trust to themselves for that; in all other things to go on in the general way as before. So every family was assigned a parcel of land, according to the proportion of their number with that in view,—for present purposes only, and making no division for inheritance,—all boys and children being included under some family. This was very successful. It made all hands very industrious, so that much more corn was planted than otherwise would have been by any means the Governor or any other could devise, and saved him a great deal of trouble, and gave far better satisfaction. The women now went willingly into the field, and took their little ones with them to plant corn, while before

---

41 William Bradford, *Of Plymouth Plantation* (first published by E. P, Button & Company in 1920; rendered into modern English, copyrighted and published by Harold Paget in 2016), 116–117.

they would allege weakness and inability; and to have compelled them would have been thought great tyranny and oppression.[42]

The assignment of individual and family stewardships among the colonists ultimately resulted in bountiful harvests that helped them repay their debts and reap the prosperity that the New World had to offer.

> *Stewards are what we need in the world today.*

Stewards are what we need in the world today. Individuals taking responsibility for not only their actions but also the resources with which they have been entrusted are more grateful and productive. If the perspective of stewardship were more prevalent in government, business, and families, there would be far less envy, ingratitude, theft, and misery.

---

42 *Of Plymouth Plantation*, 116.

9.
FINANCIAL STEWARDSHIP

"With great power there must also come--great responsibility!"

—Stan Lee[43]

"FINANCIAL STEWARDSHIP" IS not a common term when discussing money, but it should be. Many of the problems that arise from earning or inheriting wealth can trace their roots to a lack of responsibility. Holding oneself accountable to others, and at least to oneself, should be the standard when dealing with money. Having the proper perspective about wealth—and specifically considering it to be a stewardship rather than a sweepstakes fluke or an entitlement—will bring greater personal satisfaction, increased opportunities, and benefits to others.

The Harvard Business School currently offers a course titled "Nonprofit Financial Stewardship" with the program description, ". . . Designed to help managers in nonprofit organizations understand the tools, techniques, and concepts of good financial management."[44] In a family setting, isn't that something that grandparents and parents would like to accomplish with their children and grandchildren, "to help [family members] understand the tools, techniques, and concepts of good financial management"? This type of training with tools is the primary

---

43   Stan Lee, *Amazing Fantasy* (comic book), August 1962.
44   https://online-learning.harvard.edu/course/nonprofit-financial-stewardship-concepts-and-techniques-strategic-management?delta=0

function of proper planning.

Another place where you will find the term *financial stewardship* is in many Christian and Bible-based financial management courses. The principles taught in those courses are typically centered on laudable activities such as debt reduction and elimination, saving to create a safety buffer, and investing into tax-advantaged accounts, all with an emphasis on gratitude, charity, and prayer. In this chapter, we will dig a little deeper and explore some timeless truths behind financial stewardship as well as some fundamental characteristics of financial stewardship that are not typically discussed.

A vexing problem that many wealthy families encounter when estate planning is a sense of entitlement among their beneficiaries or heirs. As we have already illustrated, *entitlement* in this context is defined as the enjoyment of certain privileges without adequate responsibility. Entitled heirs want to enjoy the benefits of wealth without paying the price, and since value tends to have a direct correlation to cost, assets received at little or no cost will not necessarily be appreciated. This mentality is typically easy to identify, and it manifests itself in selfishness and complacency. I have yet to meet a client who doesn't worry about entitling family members or others when making estate plans.

Whenever value is received with little effort, there is a temptation to take it for granted.

Entitlement is not a problem restricted to immediate family relations. Whenever value is received with little effort, there is a temptation to take it for granted. I have observed the employees, friends, and even preferred charities of wealthy people exhibit entitled behavior when they have received large sums of money. While received funds won't necessarily be wasted or spent on destructive indulgences, they are at least consumed, and their value is lost forever. This reduces the chance that a lifetime of accumulated assets will have the greatest possible long-lasting, positive impact.

One of the oldest recorded literary examples of stewardship is an allegory found in the New Testament about a nobleman and his three servants. Before embarking on a long journey, the nobleman decided to entrust his servants with a significant amount of treasure, each receiving a different amount according to his abilities. Their charge was to be productive and grow the treasure as best they could.

Upon his return, the nobleman called on his servants to provide an accounting of their activities in his absence. Two of the servants presented the original treasure along with an equal amount of additional treasure (double the initial amount), which they offered back to their master. The nobleman praised them both and returned the entire treasure to his servants as a reward for their obedience and productivity. But the third servant, too afraid of losing his master's treasure, failed to participate in any gainful activity. Instead, he buried his smaller amount in the ground for safekeeping. After the servant presented his treasure intact but unmultiplied, the nobleman scolded him for his fear and inactivity. The nobleman then confiscated the treasure and sent the fearful servant away.[45]

This allegory provides some remarkable insights into stewardship. First, it is noteworthy that the nobleman does not *give* his servants his wealth as an inheritance or a bequest. The allegory says nothing of them consuming the treasure or providing a nice living for themselves. Rather, they seem to have an understanding in terms of their temporary, borrowing arrangement because they actually present their entrusted treasure, including all the gain they had earned through

---

45   Matthew 25:14–30, KJV.

investment, back to the nobleman.

Second, each servant received a different amount of treasure. The allegory doesn't explain why, but many readers interpret that the amount of entrusted talents was proportional to the investment skill and experience of the individual servants. The servant entrusted with the most treasure, for example, may have been trained and previously demonstrated competence in other financial matters. And, perhaps most importantly, his master likely had confidence in that servant's personal character, which made a larger stewardship more appropriate. The servant who controlled the least amount of treasure, on the other hand, may have had a poor track record but was still entrusted with a significant sum and an unparalleled opportunity to improve his fortunes.

Third, there was an expectation of productivity with the entrusted treasure. When the nobleman returns, he demands an accounting, and the servants present the results of their investment activities. Two of the servants were successful at growing their entrusted treasure. Though we don't know what their activities were, we can surmise that they were both actively and personally engaged in the multiplication of the treasure.

> *We are expected to be actively engaged in investing our trusted resources.*

Fourth, inactivity and passive investing of entrusted sums are not acceptable. When the third, fearful servant gives his accounting, he simply returns the original treasure to the nobleman, no more and no less. I imagine his master saying something like this: "Well, at least you could have deposited that money at the bank and earned a little interest!" But it is not enough to simply grow our money in an interest-bearing account; instead, we are expected to be actively engaged in investing our entrusted resources throughout our lives.

Finally, the purpose of the stewardships may have been primarily for the servants' personal growth and not simply to increase their master's portfolio. He left them on their own to manage those entrusted sums without any interference or assistance. The nobleman did not seem concerned with risk or the loss of his goods; he was most interested in the wise use and multiplication of the goods *by* his servants. The two faithful servants were rewarded by being able to keep the original stewardship plus the gain. The unproductive servant received no such reward; we can also assume that he received no future opportunities that may have been given to the others.

Of course, growth in investments is good, but the personal growth that can occur while engaged in that effort can provide educational experiences unlike any other. The gains from individual success can act as a springboard to future successes for the wise steward.

10.
THE THREE SPHERES OF STEWARDSHIP

> *"Nothing strengthens the judgment and quickens the conscience like individual responsibility. Nothing adds such dignity to character as the recognition of one's self-sovereignty; the right to an equal place, everywhere conceded; a place earned by personal merit, not an artificial attainment, by inheritance, wealth, family, and position."*
>
> —Elizabeth Cady Stanton[46]

AS WE AGE, generally speaking, we develop a desire to leave a lasting, positive legacy behind when we die. We do not want to burden others with our problems, we'd like to care for our immediate family and loved ones, and we'd like to benefit the community with any residual resources. These natural desires comprise the foundation of financial stewardship, but the application of that stewardship is not so intuitive: we can experience frustration trying to solve the age-old dilemma of how to properly utilize our resources ourselves and for the benefit of others.

The obligations that come with financial stewardship can be divided into three areas or spheres, ordered according to our influence and responsibility: individual, our family and loved

---

[46] Speech before the United States Senate Judiciary Committee, January 18, 1892.

ones, and then the community.

I once worked with the retired client of another advisor who had amassed more than $10 million in net worth. In spite of his financial success, the client was perhaps the most risk averse person I had ever met. While a large part of his wealth was allocated to business interests and real estate, a disproportionately large part of his assets were sitting in savings accounts and short-term treasury bills. I couldn't believe it. His millions of dollars were earning almost no interest, and what meager interest he earned was taxable and easily devoured by annual inflation.

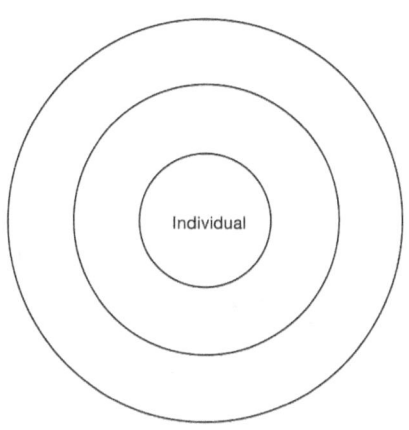

Sphere 1: Individual Stewardship

The advisor and I suggested a number of alternatives, some with strong guarantees and others with very modest risk but higher growth potential that could help grow his money. He declined every option. Decades earlier, he lost millions in a now-shuttered manufacturing company, and that experience left him with financial "scar tissue" that made him incapable of assuming any investment risk. After many unsuccessful attempts over several years, the advisor eventually gave up on helping him diversify his portfolio. Last I heard, he had still made no changes.

While some may not view this client's risk aversion as unsound—after all, he had amassed millions, albeit through real estate appreciation and saving part of his substantial income— he could have viewed his financial situation in terms of "good, better, and best." It was good that he wasn't losing any money; it would be better had he invested his funds at higher interest; and it would have been best if he had used his wealth strategically to provide for himself and provide financial opportunities to his children and the community.

When he passes, this client's wealth will transfer to his surviving spouse, who is likely to live very conservatively, as many widows do. When she dies, his children will likely equally inherit everything that is left over. It's very possible they could do beneficial things with the money, and it's also possible they will just consume that wealth as most heirs do. Because there is no strategy to provide opportunities with accountability to his children and grandchildren while he lives—and no structure to ensure that those opportunities flow to generations who come after his death—the wealth for which he toiled a lifetime has the potential to disappear in only a few short years. And he is missing out on the satisfaction of watching his family achieve even greater success during his lifetime.

Another element of individual stewardship lies in avoiding the transfer of one's personal legal and credit obligations to others. This is not only true during one's lifetime but especially at death. Legal obligations may include outstanding lawsuits, settlement liabilities, and taxes. The burden of settling other credit obligations such as consumer or property debt also shifts to the deceased's next of kin as they settle the deceased's estate. Since credit obligations may not terminate at death, many creditors require debt insurance or life insurance to assist the repayment of these obligations. Medical care prior to death can be quite expensive, and deceased people often leave behind significant medical bills for their next of kin to manage as well. Combined with the grief that surviving loved ones are already experiencing, settling a deceased estate can be a long and arduous task. We can greatly simplify our surviving loved ones' post-mortem responsibilities (and perhaps mitigate their grief) by continuously keeping our "financial house" in order and passing on as few credit or other financial obligations as possible.

Responsible people hold themselves accountable for all their actions, and part of that accountability should be for the wise accumulation and use of our financial resources. Individual stewardship over money is not only to ensure that it doesn't lose value in some harebrained scheme, but it should be invested conscientiously and carefully with a goal of multiplying the money to benefit oneself and others. When we do so, we can avoid being a burden on others and can give unparalleled opportunities to others.

Another area of stewardship is the well-being of our immediate family and loved ones. Consider this: of all the gifts you have received and resources you have accumulated, what is more precious? Our relationships with family members and loved ones are more valuable than all the riches on earth!

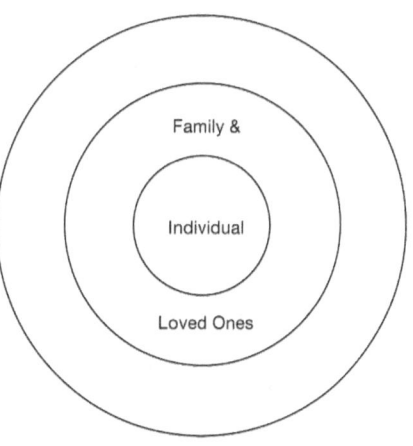

Sphere 2:
Family and Loved Ones
Stewardship

Years ago, my father fell extremely ill from an infection that nearly ended his life. He had to undergo an emergency surgery and spent several days recovering in the intensive care unit at a local hospital. After he was released, he told me that experience clarified many things for him. While he was fighting for life, not once did he wish he had spent another day at the office, enjoyed a specific leisure activity, or checked off some bucket-list item. His primary concern was his immediate family members, and *our* welfare was on his mind constantly despite his precarious circumstances. He had always been a fine example of putting his family first throughout his life, but that experience gave him even greater perspective.

> *Whose failures bring us the greatest sorrow, and whose successes bring us the greatest joy?*

Children and grandchildren, in particular, come as wondrous gifts. We nurture them, teach them, and later, they go out on their own to create their own destiny. They are ours, but only temporarily, entrusted as precious "talents" surpassing the value of all others. That being the case, in whom do we have greater interest in facilitating happiness? Whose failures bring us the greatest sorrow, and whose successes bring us the greatest joy?

I have often observed retirees pack up their homes from their childbearing years and move to warmer weather. Many spend their days golfing, visiting the spa, researching long-lost ancestors, and engaging in other stimulating or relaxing activities. They have worked hard to get to where they are, and they deserve some diversion. But what if more retirees added an additional item to their retirement "job description," one that would bring greater satisfaction than all those other activities combined? What if they made greater effort to share their wisdom and directly invest in the financial success of their children and grandchildren?

The problem is that most people are perplexed about how to invest in and help their family members financially during their lifetime. The desire to help is there, but the proper way to help usually isn't clear. Giving money away with no strings attached can cause the giver concern if the funds are not used as expected. Making stipulations on the proper use of funds can feel overbearing to the receiver, and the receiver may resent the giver. Many simply give up after a few attempts to help backfire.

When it comes to those who have tried and failed to assist their loved ones financially, I like to invite them to rethink their methods of assistance. Helping loved ones in the Family Bank system is not a one-way street; it is actually a partnership capitalizing on and sharing the respective strengths of each partner. Older family members can benefit financially and emotionally from their collaboration with younger family members. When speaking with retired clients, for example, I like to emphasize the potential benefits of one generation working with another by asking the following: "Generally speaking, what do young people lack?" A good answer could be "wealth and experience" since those tend to be the fruits of a lifetime of work. "Generally speaking, what do older people lack?" Age typically brings a loss of youthful energy and health.

In the Family Bank system, generations are drawn together by mutually beneficial financial arrangements. When funding these arrangements, older people effectively borrow their children's and grandchildren's health and youth, and the younger generation is able to borrow their parents' and grandparents' maturity and success. What a beautiful contrast to the generational tension that one often sees in the family setting! Young people cease to be resentful of their more successful older relatives, and older relatives don't look down on their less experienced younger relatives. In the Family Bank, they work together, invest in the success of each other, and enjoy greater respect and love for each other.

> *Generations are drawn together by mutually beneficial financial arrangements.*

I often imagine how much greater, positive impact the younger generation could have on the world if the older generation could help alleviate the burden of financial stress. Many young people have postponed a passion or field of interest in favor of financial stability. Many remarkable ideas for products and services were never launched because their creators lacked funding capital. If more families and groups practiced the principles and had access to the tools of the Family Bank, there could be remarkable breakthroughs in technology, medicine, and transportation, just to name a few.

> *There could be remarkable breakthroughs in technology, medicine, and transportation, just to name a few.*

There is an old saying in our industry that if you don't spend your retirement money on cruises and golf outings, your children will. But is it best to just spend the money yourself? You get to the point where there is only so much house you can live in, only so many clothes you can wear, only so many cars you can drive, and only so much food you can eat. Many retirees seek something more meaningful. Why not be engaged in the most satisfying work there is: teaching, guiding, and rewarding your family members to work and grow, all while providing them and future generations the tools to do so in your absence?

Finally, financial stewardship is also interconnected with our communities and the larger world around us. Once we are meeting our stewardship obligations to ourselves and our loved ones, it is natural to wish to benefit our fellow citizens. Many hospitals, museums, college campuses, and other facilities or nonprofit organizations bear the name of generous benefactors who donated money intended to help others. Every client with a considerable estate that I have worked with has also expressed a particular desire to help the less fortunate.

A question that often preoccupies intellectuals and philanthropists is this: "How should we *help* the less fortunate around us?" The trouble comes in figuring out the best way to extend that assistance since some well-meaning efforts or offerings can be the means of creating greater harm. I don't know of anyone who thinks it's a good idea to offer cash gifts to those with addictions, for example. Thus, the real question is "What is the *best* way to help others?"

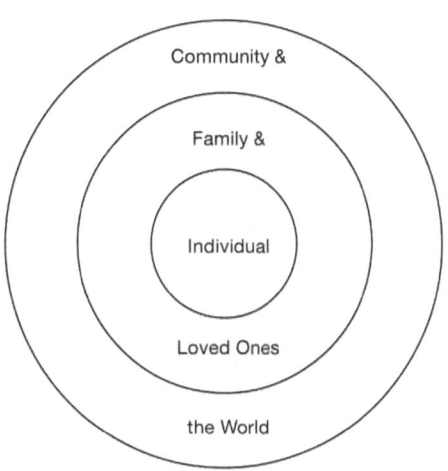

Sphere 3: Community Stewardship

When I was younger, my parents often took our family downtown for family activities. Museums and shopping malls were our favorite venues, and we mostly walked around for a few hours before children were sufficiently exhausted and ready for bed. As is common in most major cities, we encountered several homeless people with signs asking for food or money. My parents are some of the most generous people I know, but we never knew how they would respond to such requests. Sometimes they gave a few coins, bills, or food vouchers; other times, they simply ignored the request. A few times, we invited homeless people to join our family for a meal at the local food court. Several times, my father even offered temporary employment at our home and yard.

On one occasion, I remember asking my parents why they didn't always give money to homeless people on the street. They responded that they weren't sure how the money would be spent, and they didn't want to facilitate any self-abusive behavior by funding the purchase of drugs or alcohol. It was a fair concern, but it seemed unfair to withhold money from the needy.

> *Trying to help the needy can be a classic no-win situation.*

Most people have witnessed a similar scene many times during their lifetime. Many of us certainly wanted to help but were unsure how. We have given out cash in some instances and wondered if we just hurt the person by funding a destructive vice. We have turned our heads at other times, pretending not to see the request for help, walking or driving away with a degree of shame or guilt for ignoring a desperate plea. This classic no-win situation presents a very raw dilemma for those who would like to benefit the less fortunate but worry about actually hurting them.

Some respond that it's up to the less fortunate to lift themselves out of their indigent circumstances. After all, we live in a free country where we have greater opportunities to achieve than anywhere else, regardless of the circumstances we're born into. While this is possible, my experience has shown this is less probable. There are only a few well-known examples of those who have overcome their impoverished circumstances to enjoy prosperity. Occasionally we hear of some famous person or athlete who rose from poverty to make millions, yet millions of others in similar situations remain exactly where they are, and usually for the rest of their lives. Sadly, the trajectory from poverty to prosperity is the exception instead of the rule. More often than not, generations of families live and die in the same impoverished circumstances.

Wouldn't it be nice if we could reverse those results and make poverty the exception rather than the rule? Others respond that we should donate greater sums to charity or "invest" more taxpayer dollars into education, affordable housing, job training, medical treatment, and other federal and state programs. While an estimated $22 trillion[47] has been spent since President Lyndon B. Johnson announced his seminal "war on poverty" in 1964, the average percentage of the US population living below the poverty line has changed little.[48] President Johnson's goal ". . . not only to relieve the symptom of poverty, but to cure it and, above all, to prevent it" has not been accomplished, despite trillions in spending and decades of effort.

Our community stewardship certainly does not bid us to *hurt* anyone, but are we really *helping* when we just throw money at problems? Is that the best way to *help*?

> *Are we really helping when we just throw money at problems?*

---

47 https://www.forbes.com/sites/louiswoodhill/2014/03/19/the-war-on-poverty-wasnt-a-failure-it-was-a-catastrophe/?sh=601b58fc6f49
48 https://www.census.gov/content/dam/Census/library/publications/2020/demo/p60-270.pdf

11.

TRAINING *WITH* TOOLS

"I get by with a little help from my friends."

—John Lennon & Paul McCartney[49]

WHAT, THEN, IS the best way to help others? A popular response is the old, familiar adage about fishing and human nature: "Give a man a fish, and he'll eat for a day; teach a man to fish, and he'll eat for a lifetime." Training people to take care of themselves is a noble aspiration, but a little visualization reveals that this adage is woefully incomplete.

> The old adage of "teach a man to fish" is woefully incomplete.

Imagine a young man in tattered clothing standing beside a river. He is thin, and water is dripping from his ragged clothes. His hunger has obliged him to plunge into the river for food, yet each dive yields no fish. His clumsy hands are simply no match for the fish's natural instincts and fins. He pulls himself from the river repeatedly without success.

Then imagine an experienced fisherman upstream observing this pathetic scene. He reels in his line and walks down the

---

49   John Lennon and Paul McCartney, "With a Little Help from My Friends," 1967.

riverbank toward the hungry man. In one hand is a basket with several fish he has successfully harvested for himself and his family. As he approaches the man, he feels deep sympathy and opens the basket. He looks down at the fish that could easily satiate the young man's hunger. But he hesitates and considers the consequences of that act. He says to the hungry man, "If I give you a fish, your hunger will disappear. But it will come back tomorrow, and I won't be here when it does. I need these fish to feed my family. May I teach you to fish instead? Then you'll be able to feed yourself from now on."

The hungry man enthusiastically agrees, and the old fisherman proceeds to instruct him how to fish. He informs him of where to stand, what parts of the river contain fish, and when they are likely to bite. He shows him his rod and reel as well as various hooks, lures, and other tackle. He demonstrates how to cast a line into the river and gives the hungry man an opportunity to try on his own. After ensuring the hungry man has listened well and demonstrated understanding, he thanks him for his attention and bids him adieu. "Best of luck to you," the fisherman says as he leaves the riverbank and walks home.

What is the problem with this scene? Without the proper fishing tackle, the hungry man is physically no better off than he was before he met the fisherman. Though he has been given valuable knowledge and experience he could use to greatly benefit himself and others, he has no way of improving his situation *without the proper tools*.

The hungry man is no better off than he was before he learned to fish.

Let's imagine two alternate endings to this scene.

Ending #1: What if the fisherman just gave the man his tackle?

Presumably, the fisherman could be harming *himself* because he donated the very means of providing for himself and his family. Yes, the hungry man's situation would improve, but at what cost? Also, assuming the tackle has some secondhand value, what is to prevent the hungry man from pawning it instead of using it to catch fish? And what if the hungry man suffered from an unhealthy gambling habit or another vice? He could potentially use that money to indulge that vice and possibly lose the money all together. Without the right discipline and planning, the value of the tackle could be lost forever.

Ending #2: What if the fisherman *lent* his tackle to the hungry man?

The fisherman loans the hungry man his tackle and then sets the following terms: "Bring me five fish each day to feed my family, and additional fish you catch belong to you. If you catch more fish than you need, you can take the rest to market and sell them for money. Save that money to purchase your own tackle. Make this your only work. Avoid any expenses or diversions that would devour your savings. Within thirty days, you should have enough to buy your own tackle. Then come and return my tackle to me at my home. After that, go and make your living."

Imagine a happy reunion thirty days later. The hungry man is now well-fed, and he has mastered his new occupation. He is wearing new clothes and brings back the old fisherman's tackle clean and functional. He also proudly shows the new tackle he has been able to purchase through his hard work and saving. With tears in his eyes, he embraces the old fisherman and thanks him for his generosity.

The old fisherman smiles and shakes his head. "Friend, this is how I learned to be a fisherman. I was like you many years ago—hungry and hopeless. A kind fisherman had compassion on me in my hour of need. He did the same things that I did with you. He taught me to fish and loaned me his tackle. He believed in me and told me I would succeed. He saved my life. When I asked how I could ever repay him, he told me if I ever saw another hungry man to pass on this great wisdom. Now I pass his invitation on to you: when you encounter another in need like you were, go and do likewise."

I have yet to hear anyone repeat that old fishing adage about "teaching a man to fish" and include, "*and* give him access to the proper tackle," but tools are just as critical as training. Not only did the wise, old fisherman give the hungry man an opportunity to catch fish under his supervision, but he gave him extended opportunities to exercise that training by himself for thirty days. Training by itself often goes in one ear and out the other, but hands-on experience with tools can be impossible to forget.

Tools are just as critical as training.

Education alone cannot generate success; it must be coupled with experience and tools through supervision by those who have already realized success. Granting extended access to the proper financial tools can empower people to achieve greatness and help others.

12.

COMPASSIONATE CAPITALISM

"Capitalism undoubtedly has certain boils and blotches upon it, but has it as many as government? Has it as many as marriage? Has it as many as religion? I doubt it. It is the only basic institution of modern man that shows any genuine health and vigor."

—H. L. Mencken[50]

A REAL-WORLD EXAMPLE of proper financial tools improving lives today can be found in some of the poorest countries on earth. This "hand up" at the individual level can create more lasting improvement as opposed to the billions in massive "handouts" provided by wealthy nations, individuals, and charities.

Years ago, a client invited me to learn more about a microloan organization with whom he had become closely affiliated. He billed the underlying effort as the best self-motivated solution for poverty. He called it "compassionate capitalism," and I wanted to learn more. At a monthly meeting, the group showed a video of impoverished but optimistic entrepreneurs in Bangladesh. It was inspiring to see the creative products they produced.

One woman had an idea to prepare and sell delicious sausages made from discarded bits of meat the city's butchers donated to her. She had perfected a recipe and knew she would find plenty

---

50   *American Mercury* (founded in 1924, now an online magazine), August 1928.

of customers to purchase her snack. But she had no funds to purchase a street cart or fuel for cooking.

A local Bangladeshi bank, financed by a US-based microloan funding organization, offered to loan the woman the equivalent of $100 to purchase a cart and cooking supplies. I recall the interest rate was quite high, maybe 20 percent annually. But she was grateful and eager to work. In no time, she had accumulated enough income to repay the loan, purchase a larger street cart, and employ an assistant. Most importantly, she now had enough money to feed her children, purchase clothes and books for them, and pay for their schooling. She was determined to break the cycle of poverty in which she had grown up, and all she needed was the financial means to realize her dream.

There are a few characteristics of typical microloans worth mentioning:

1. Loans are in small denominations. Microloans are typically a few hundred dollars or less, hence the defining word micro. They cater specifically to extremely impoverished individuals for whom that amount of money can be life changing.

2. Down payments are sometimes required. Loan candidates usually have to demonstrate the ability to save a percentage of the loan being offered.

3. Loan candidates must have a specific profile. In this case, the bank would usually offer loans only to women. After observing men often waste their loan money on alcohol, gambling, and brothels, banks made a practice of lending almost exclusively to women, particularly mothers. Mothers were found to be more motivated to succeed than single men, and their repayments were more reliable. Why? Mothers' priority was providing

food, clothing, shelter, and schooling for their children. Strong motivations to succeed more often ensured that the interest and loans would be repaid.

Living in one of the wealthiest nations on earth shields us from the desperate poverty that is so common worldwide. Even though the monetary amounts are different in every situation, the same principles for financial self-improvement apply to everyone. We have the capacity to improve our situation with hard work, proper management, and the right financial tools. Having access to cash through savings or financing tends to make the biggest difference between success and failure. It's the "capital" in *capitalism*—that is the key to helping people change their destiny.

Though our family and community contexts may be different, the same methods of promoting self-reliance and opportunity can radically improve the destinies of our family members, loved ones, and others in our communities. Providing access to the right tools to achieve these outcomes is an act of wisdom and compassion.

13.

THREE INGREDIENTS FOR FINANCIAL SUCCESS

"Money is none of the wheels of trade: it is the oil which renders the motion of the wheels more smooth and easy."

—David Hume[51]

HAVE YOU EVER wanted to be a millionaire or billionaire? Most of us have daydreamed at some point about having more money than we know what to do with. But simply possessing and consuming lots of money will eventually come to an end; just look at most lottery winners and the descendants of Industrial Age billionaire families who have nothing today. So, what would *you* do with that much money? And how would you make sure your money keeps growing?

To make as much money as a millionaire or billionaire, you must think like one. More importantly, you must invest and manage your money like one. And don't think you are precluded from imitating their management style because you have far fewer financial resources; you can do the exact same thing they do regardless of the amount of money you have.

Unlike most investors, you won't typically see the super wealthy purchasing the kinds of investments and products that are advertised on the radio, television, internet, or by

---

51   David Hume, "Of Money," *Essays: Moral and Political* (1741–1742).

most financial advisors. Millionaires and billionaires don't pay attention to loudmouth stock peddlers in some faraway cable news studio, nor do they listen to HR personnel and financial advisors recommending retirement funds the advisors know next to nothing about. They certainly don't let their emotions get stirred by zealous neighbors or salespeople spinning fairy tales of impossible returns in so-called "investment opportunities." No, they are more strategic and informed in their investments than most people, and they can realize much higher returns because of it. It could be real estate, troubled businesses, booming businesses, or whatever the wealthy investor has a particular talent for or interest in.

From closely observing several billionaires and dozens of multi-millionaire families, business owners, and entrepreneurs throughout my career, I have noticed that the super wealthy possess three resources that make their investment and management work successful:

1. An idea, skill, or product that others want. It must be marketable and accessible to others in exchange for money.

2. Business acumen. The person must be willing to work hard to create, package, and distribute the good or service efficiently and affordably. The business owner must be adept in navigating the complexities of accounting systems, supply chains, marketing, taxes, employee relations, and so on.

3. Capital. This final ingredient is the primary, limited resource in achieving financial success. Without it, many of the greatest innovations and hardest workers would have been relegated to obscurity. In many cases I have encountered, entrepreneurs and

> *Capital is the primary, limited resource in achieving financial success.*

workers usually lacked the financial resources to get their idea off the ground or expand their businesses; many had to enter into some kind of funding arrangement to proceed.

The world is teeming with hardworking people with great ideas for services or products they could sell, but most of those never get off the ground because of a lack of capital. Most of the successful people I have met aren't smarter or harder working than others; they simply had access to capital at crucial moments that made the difference. They still had to use the funds properly and be wise business operators, but the successful people I have met got ahead by having access to cash when others didn't.

The world is teeming with hardworking people with great ideas, but most of those never get off the ground because of a lack of capital.

There are typically only three sources of capital for business enterprises. Let me analyze the advantages and disadvantages of each:

1) Self-funding.

This means using savings or other liquid assets to fund the new enterprise. It usually involves tax consequences and lost opportunity cost. Few people or corporations keep large sums of cash lying around; those who do typically earn next to nothing in traditional bank accounts, and whatever interest they earn is taxable each year. With annual inflation reducing that cash's buying power, the net effect of large savings accounts or their equivalents is actually to *lose* money. The cash could be better stored elsewhere, but most don't know where the best place is.

Another method of self-funding I have observed on the individual level is premature distributions from retirement plans. I have seen entrepreneurs drain their 401(k) accounts or IRAs and take a painful tax hit. Not only are those plan distributions subject to ordinary income tax, but there is an additional 10 percent penalty for those under age fifty-nine and a half. Depending on their tax brackets, they could potentially see a tax loss of 30 to 50 percent of their account value when liquidating it. Plus, they vlose the potential growth of those retirement accounts in the future. That is definitely expensive funding.

The last method of self-funding on the individual level I have observed is what I call the "yard sale." This consists of selling jewelry, furniture, or other assets that can be converted to cash, usually at a loss. It's true that success often demands sacrifice, but it's demoralizing to see your possessions disappear, especially those that have family or sentimental significance. I don't believe the common regret associated with this kind of self-funding is worth it.

2) Debt contracts.

This is a common means of securing funding for business ventures. There are many financial institutions (such as banks) as well as wealthy individuals or groups who are in a position to loan funds for almost any purpose. The cost of that obligation is typically interest, and the interest charged is directly related to the owner or corporation's credit rating, collateral, and track record for success.

Unfortunately, many new businesses fail, and that interest cost and risk of failure applies constant pressure on the new business. According to the Bureau of Labor Statistics in 2020, approximately 22 percent of new businesses failed during the first year of being opened, 46 percent during the first five years, and 66 percent during the first ten years.[52] Only 25 percent of new businesses make it to fifteen years or more.

Besides using business loans, I have seen business owners find cash by mortgaging properties like players in the game of Monopoly. They refinance their homes, take out second mortgages or home equity lines of credit (HELOC), or enter into personal property loans at high interest rates. Debt is a merciless business partner that never sleeps, takes vacations, or forgets what you owe. And debt is first in line to collect if you fail.

> *Debt is a merciless business partner that never sleeps, takes vacations, or forgets what you owe.*

3) Ownership sales.

This is the last common way of generating capital for businesses that I will mention. If you have ever paid attention to a company "going public" through an "initial public offering" (IPO), you have just observed a corporation sell its ownership to generate revenue. This can be a significant payday for the former owners, but it abandons complete control of the company. On the small business or individual side, many business owners must contract with investors or institutions to sell a significant ownership stake in exchange for funding to get an idea off the ground. Depending on the percentage sale and the relationship dynamics of the multiple owners, it could create conflict and frustration. Quantitatively, the effect of this premature sale is proportional when the original owner sells a successful business years down the road: he or she will stand to make millions instead

---

52 https://www.bls.gov/bdm/us_age_naics_00_table7.txt

of tens or hundreds of millions.

Those with access to capital are typically able to realize greater success than those without their same resources. Those with fast access to cash are able to add zeros to the size of their transactions, and those successful returns are proportionately larger thanks to their capital funding.

14.
THE FAMILY BANK

*"The love of wealth is therefore to be traced,
as either a principal or an accessory motive,
at the bottom of all that the Americans do;
this gives to all their passions a sort of family likeness."*

—Alexis de Tocqueville[53]

THE IDEAL SOURCE of capital funding for life-changing activities such as education, home purchases, and business creation or expansion is the Family Bank. Even though many may be unfamiliar with the term "Family Bank," we have discussed how the principles behind it are ancient; in fact, they are timeless. Some who have already heard about Family Banks have possibly read one of only a handful of books or articles out there attempting to describe it. Much of what they describe is actually a "family vault" where money is stored, waiting to be doled out for specific purposes and often distributed equally among heirs at death. The limited structure they describe is unlikely to continuously grow the family fortune and benefit the lives of countless descendants and others.

Instead of a vault, I like to think of the Family Bank as a campfire. Imagine that the logs represent the assets and

Instead of a vault, the Family Bank is like a campfire.

---

53   Alexis de Tocqueville, *Democracy in America*, Vol, 2, Sec. 3, Chapter 21, Henry Reeve, trans.(1840).)

money that are available to family members and others. The fire is what these individuals do with the wealth; whether it is constructive or destructive depends on what controls are in place. A trained hand can use fire to cook food, power vehicles, and provide many lifesaving and even luxurious services. A careless hand can let the fire get out of control and destroy forests, property, and even lives.

> *Logs bundled in a fire will burn hotter and longer than if the logs were separated.*

If the burning logs in a campfire are removed and separated from each other, each log will stay lit temporarily and then flame out into smoke. That is the end of the usefulness of the fuel, and the useful flames and heat can be lost forever. But if the logs are kept burning together in a bundle, the fire will burn hotter and longer than if the logs were separated. New logs and tinder can systematically replace the old, and the fire can burn forever if it is properly managed. A burning torch or other tinder can also be carefully transported to illuminate other tinder in other locations that can become roaring campfires themselves.

Families with a Family Bank treat money with the same care as one should treat a fire. As mentioned before, making loans, not gifts, is one of the keys to making the Family Bank function and survive. Besides the preferred legacy assets inside the Family Bank, loans from the family wealth keep it from being dissipated. These loans not only maintain the family fortune, but they can even grow it. Without the division and consumption of assets that often occurs when individual heirs receive an inheritance, family wealth can remain indefinitely inside the Family Bank because it is not owned by *any one* person. This can protect family members from themselves, as well as curtail outside opportunists or other threats to the family fortune.

Distributions from the Family Bank generally fall into three categories: loans, grants, and gifts. Each has different purposes and requirements.

LOANS

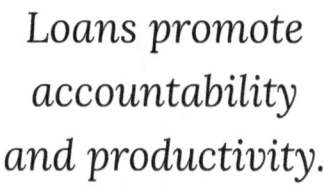

Loans promote accountability and productivity.

Loans create accountability that protects family members and the Family Bank alike. While gifts to heirs tend to create consumers, loans can create stewards. When heirs know that money entrusted to them must be returned, they are less likely to waste it. When there is a required repayment plan with interest attached to the loan, heirs are more likely to be industrious with the loaned funds.

Family members are generally preapproved for a loan. Those seeking funding are required to bring a proposal to the Family Bank for consideration. A "bank board" made of family members or professionals can approve loans and arrange repayment schedules tailored to the individual and the circumstances of the loan. Unlike commercial banks, care for the individual and rapid approval should be hallmarks of the Family Bank. Examples of industrious uses for loan money may include schooling, housing, business creation or expansion, or other investments. Family members who make profits from these activities repay their loans but are welcome to keep the gain for themselves. These gains can be the means of future investment activities financed without the help of the Family Bank.

GRANTS

The Family Bank may also provide non-loan grants to assist family members with medical expenses, disabilities, or other difficulties. Unfortunately, some are afflicted with physical challenges that require help from others. For example, medical support for serious illnesses and disabilities can be quite expensive and beyond the financial resources of some family members. By providing support funds, families with a Family Bank are more empowered to take care of themselves and less reliant on government or charitable services to help family members with those challenges.

Grants can fund developmental activities without repayment.

The Family Bank may also fund certain developmental and charitable activities for family members through grants. Many families enjoy engaging in a variety of educational, service, and religious activities, and the Family Bank can serve as a benefactor instead of a creditor since cash grants may be preferable for these types of activities. Annual donations to charities of the family members' choice can be distributed as well. As long as assets are growing inside the Family Bank, these types of distributions can come from gains without depleting the Family Bank's resources.

GIFTS

It should be stated that some gifts to family and friends are perfectly acceptable. Every Family Bank will have to find the right balance. Note that some gifts may be taxable to the receiver. We all love presents for holidays, birthdays, and other special events, and they tend to bring joy to both giver and receiver alike. Parents and grandparents know their children and grandchildren best and often enjoy giving gifts that family members could not acquire on their own. Some gifting of business interests to the next generation may be appropriate for those working in the family business according to a contractual agreement. Congratulatory gifts, such as funding a marriage or rewarding a college graduation, may also be appropriate. A guiding principle for gifting by parents and grandparents could be this: "Only give what you are prepared to have consumed."

Those who create a Family Bank are able to bypass the traditional banking system and take care of and provide enriching opportunities to their family members. Rather than enriching commercial bankers or brokers, families with this planning tool have their resources pooled for individual opportunities linked with accountability. There is no limit to what can be achieved by industrious people who have access to the right resources at the right time.

> *"Only give what you are prepared to have consumed."*

15.
THE TROUBLE WITH DIRECT LOANS

"The holy passion of Friendship is of so sweet and steady and loyal and enduring a nature that it will last through a Whole Lifetime, if not asked to lend money."

—Mark Twain[54]

A COMMON RESPONSE I have received when presenting the Family Bank is this: "Why do I need a trust or other legal entity to act like a Family Bank? Can't I just loan money directly to my kids and grandkids on my own?" Of course, the answer is yes, and many family members and others make direct loans to each other every day. There are many success stories of people receiving loans directly from friends or relatives in the right way and saving thousands in interest. I have seen parents and grandparents successfully assist family members with education, home purchases, and other financial enterprises where they made significant gains from family loans. But we all know stories—or we may even have a few personal stories of our own—where direct loans were never fully repaid and the transaction kindled strife between lender and borrower.

The obvious advantage of direct loans for the borrower is the opportunity to bypass the traditional financial "underwriting"

---

54 Mark Twain, *Pudd'nhead Wilson*, Chapter 9 (1894).

process that occurs when a bank or other lending institution considers a loan applicant's request. Banks typically require bank statements, tax returns, credit scores, income verification, and collateral information, among other things. Institutions may also charge a higher interest rate that applicants hope to avoid by relying on the generosity of their family relations or friendships. For their part, the family members and loved ones who lend are motivated by a desire to help and are willing to assume the higher risk and lower return from making a private loan.

The trouble with direct loans is that they can create unintended consequences that negatively affect one's relationships, not to mention one's finances. I have seen quite a few horror stories arise from loans between family members that were unclear, repaid late, or even defaulted. Often, the root of these problems lies in lenders failing to draw up formal legal agreements with the borrower or failing to properly enforce the terms of the loan. Even when something is written down and signed, misinterpretations and misunderstandings of the agreement can create enmity between the two parties.

Misinterpretations and misunderstandings of the agreement can create enmity between the two parties.

For those insistent on making direct loans to family members and loved ones, I recommend approaching such loans in the same way a bank does.[55] Even though most private lending arrangements do not get close to emulating this process, here are a few tips to keep in mind at a minimum:

- Never loan more than you can afford to lose

---

55 https://www.finra.org/investors/insights/lending-friends-and-family

- Always charge interest
- Always charge an appropriate interest rate (depending on the loan, the Internal Revenue Service requires minimum interest rate between private parties; see "Gift" tax rules and current "Applicable Federal Rate" or "AFR")
- Always have a written, signed contract with a repayment schedule

While it is possible to make direct, personal loans work (and in a perfect world, everyone would act responsibly to make them work), the risks to relationships from loans can be easily reduced and transferred to a third party for relatively little cost and effort. In the same way that we purchase insurance to repair or replace our homes, vehicles, and income, the financial and relationship risk from direct loans can be "outsourced" by tasking that function to a third party. This third party can act as an intermediary between family members and loved ones to alleviate any contention or awkwardness the lender and borrower may experience in connection to the loan.

The ideal third party in this example can be the Family Bank. The trustee(s) or other administrators from the Family Bank can effectively replace wealthier family members to provide funds to the borrower with their money but without the hassle. In some cases, it may be best for the parent or relative who sets up the trust with his or her money to *not even know* the particulars of an applicant's loan or interaction with the trustee(s).

Create a "Thanksgiving Protection Plan."

Another good reason for establishing a Family Bank is to preclude any awkward conversations with family members or others who make requests for money. How nice would it be *not* to have financial issues between family members affect relationships and family gatherings? I call this the "Thanksgiving Protection Plan."

Parents and grandparents can establish boundaries in financial matters with other family members without the perception of favoritism or personal rejection. If a child asks for a loan, grant, or gift from a parent, for example, the parent can simply direct the child to the administrators of the Family Bank for such requests. The parent could respond, "Great! I've already set up a way to do that through the Family Bank. Jim and Carol are taking care of things in that area, and they will help you with what you need." Further, if the child were to fall behind on loan repayments or default on a loan, the controversy of that delicate situation is between the family member and the Family Bank, not between a child and the parent.

A final reason for establishing a Family Bank as opposed to direct loans is perpetuity: Family Banks have the ability to outlive their founders by design. The legal structure of Family Banks (to be discussed in the following chapter) can continually grow assets and enable low-interest loans to be available for multiple, successive generations. The same principles of hard work and stewardship that successful family members embody can be passed on to each subsequent generation of descendants or other beneficiaries.

How nice would it be to take advantage of lower interest rates and minimal underwriting requirements of a direct loan from a family member without risk of it affecting relationships? How great would it be for family applicants to enjoy the benefits of low-interest money without threatening the peace of holidays and family gatherings? The Family Bank provides the ideal solution.

16.
CREATING THE INFRASTRUCTURE

*"If you have built castles in the air,
your work need not be lost; that is where they should be.
Now put the foundations under them."*

—Henry David Thoreau[56]

IN THIS CHAPTER, we will explore some of the details of the Family Bank that may be more esoteric than enlightening. While this will not be an exhaustive presentation of all the legal and tax issues impacting the Family Bank, I will mention some important highlights that families should consider when they are trying to create a framework for their own Family Bank.

First, I must clarify something: Some have understood the Family Bank to be a specific kind of trust or another legal or business entity owned by a family or established for the benefit of its members. The Family Bank would be rather mundane and soulless if that were all it was. While it is true that Family Banks must have a set legal structure to endure for multiple generations (and I highly recommend adopting that structure when necessary), legal structure is not what creates or defines a Family Bank. Many

At the heart of the Family Bank are two things: love and money.

---
56   Henry David Thoreau, *Walden*, Chapter 18 (1854).

in the world are already practicing the principles of the Family Bank by prudently offering direct, low-interest loans to family members or others (as we explored in the previous chapter). The prominent families who have employed the protections and enhancements of trusts, partnerships, and corporations have used them *as tools* to "institutionalize" their Family Bank, but those entities are *not* the Family Bank. No, at the heart of the Family Bank are actually two things far simpler and quite effectual: love and money.

Love is what motivates people to create Family Banks—pure and simple. All parents want their children to succeed, and many would like to help their children avoid some of the difficult experiences they have gone through caused by limited financial resources. Just as love often compels people to make strong commitments to each other, successful individuals establishing Family Banks make a conscious commitment to assisting other family members during their lifetimes and beyond by sharing their financial success strategically.

Besides love, *money* is also what makes a Family Bank possible. Without money, family members may be limited in their power to help each other. Parents generally try to save a little money here and there to assist their children in the future. Those with greater financial resources, like grandparents and others who are usually "chronologically gifted" as I like to call them, also tend to care deeply about their younger family members and desire to help them achieve independence and success. Money can make incredible things happen in a family when used properly. But when there's money without the proper financial principles and practices, money can be a burden and can even facilitate self-destructive behavior in some.

Many families have already thought through many of the issues we have explored and have already done a fair amount of planning to avoid such problems. While only a few families have created a Family Bank structure that goes on perpetually, significant changes to their existing plan may not be necessary in order to do so. Indeed, drastic changes are often improbable since they are likely to be costly and time-consuming.

> *Significant changes to your plan may not be necessary.*

Depending on the size of the estate and the planning that has already been done, existing wills, trusts, and other legal entities can be modified with "amendments" or other modifications to create the legal structure for the Family Bank. Certain assets can also be "earmarked" specifically for the Family Bank.

Asset transfer into such entities can occur immediately, over time, or at death, depending on one's individual circumstances. The existing team of legal and tax advisors may be able to make changes or draft additional estate documents. In some cases, specialists may need to assist.

Deciding how much of one's estate should be "earmarked" for the Family Bank is a concept we will explore in a later chapter. Depending on that amount—and how large an estate a person has—there will likely be tax considerations that must be a part of the planning. The federal estate tax has changed many times over the years, and it could add up to a significant amount depending on the size of the estate. Needless to say, both objectives can be accomplished simultaneously.

Since they have the longest-lasting legal precedence with this type of planning, trusts are the basic and most common legal structure that can institutionalize your Family Bank for generations. Trusts act as an extension of a person's life and assets, an undying shadow of those desirous to direct the proper use of their residual resources in their absence. People who create trusts with the help of legal counsel are called *grantors*. Trusts can include a wide variety of creative language and provisions to reflect the desires (and whims) of grantors.

Those given the responsibility to carry out the grantor's wishes as spelled out in the trust are called *trustees*. Many trusts make the grantor(s) the trustee(s), and some trustees may be relatives. Some trustees can also be wholly unrelated, such as attorneys, banks, or dedicated trust institutions. Often, trusts will name *successor trustees* who can manage the trust's affairs if trustees die, retire, or are disqualified from serving as trustees. It's helpful to create provisions that allow additional trustees to be added later.

Those able to benefit from the resources and management of the trust are called *beneficiaries*. Most of the time, a trust's beneficiaries are declared at the time the trust is established, but provisions can and should be added to the trust to be able to add or even remove other beneficiaries later. Beneficiaries of a trust are often the direct family members of the grantor, but they can include a variety of other individuals or institutions as well. From here, I will refer to family members and others named as beneficiaries of the trusts as *members*.

Although there are several distinct kinds of trusts that currently work well with the Family Bank, certain trusts tend to come in and out of fashion for varied reasons. Two big reasons are taxation and regulation, and sometimes the purpose or process of a trust can be immediately reversed by legislation or litigation. Since there is pending legislation to modify the operation and taxation of many grantor trusts at the time of this writing, I will simply mention that *irrevocable* "dynasty" trusts have traditionally been the best legal vehicle to consolidate and store assets designated for the Family Bank strategy. They have historically helped families distribute assets to heirs and plan for and pay estate taxes. Remember that taxes must not be overlooked while setting up the Family Bank.

Partnerships and corporations can also be helpful entities for conducting Family Bank operations. Depending on the current laws, these entities could perform the same function as a trust and be perpetuated for generations. The ownership and control of these entities is key to the taxation and regulation of assets within these entities, and competent tax and legal counsel are best suited to describe their function and help you decide if they are right for you.

17.

THE BANK BOARD

"Experto credite." [Believe an expert.]

—Virgil[57]

AS MENTIONED IN a previous chapter, trustees are generally responsible for the administrative and fiduciary functions of the assets owned by the Family Bank. The terms "bank board" or "board of trustees" are often used to describe these individuals and others who are charged with benefitting the trust's beneficiaries and assisting in the management of legacy assets, such as real estate and certain cash equivalent accounts. They fulfill the crucial task of making low-interest loans available to family members and others for approved activities. These bank board members may also advise in the management of corporations, partnerships, and foundations outside of the trust besides carrying out their duties as trustees and properly educating family members in matters of finance.

Often, the most valuable assets held by wealthy families are businesses and real estate associated with those businesses. The Family Bank may not be the best owner of such assets. Nonpublic, family-held businesses, for example, tend to be run and owned by individuals (or other business entities owned by individuals) for operational and tax reasons. While Family Banks could potentially own profit-earning business entities,

---

57   *Aeneid,* Book 2, Line 283.

managerial control of those businesses could be complicated if executive power rests on trustees who have other responsibilities and may have less experience in a particular business sector. Also, the traditionally high federal tax rate of trust income would oblige the Family Bank to offset that income with distributions to trust beneficiaries or donations to charity each year, contrary to the Family Bank's practice of eschewing gifting and entitlements.

Real estate and cash equivalent assets tend to be the preferred choice of Family Banks. David Rockefeller once confirmed his family's lack of business holdings in their Family Bank:

> The wealth in our family, of course, came out of the oil business, of Standard Oil, but the business hasn't kept us together and there are many families who it's pulled apart, frankly. By chance, I think, we were lucky that we didn't have a business that was pulling us apart. We had a business that supplied—through generation-skipping trust—wealth that went down through the generations and dispersed through more and more people, but still was retained. But we didn't have a core business.[58]

Family members may purchase ownership in family businesses through low-interest loans from their Family Bank.

Family members may be able to purchase ownership in family businesses or other interests with assistance from low-interest loans from the Family Bank, but that may be the extent of the bank board's involvement in family business interests.

Because of the training

---

58   https://www.cnbc.com/2018/03/26/david-rockefeller-jr-shares-4-secrets-to-wealth-and-family.html

and administrative responsibilities associated with the bank board, it is prudent that its members have excellent credentials and training. Besides having applicable educational degrees and professional experience, it is best for some family members to be among the directors or on the board of trustees to ensure the continuity of the family's traditions and interests inside the Family Bank. Indeed, those who grew up learning and experimenting with tools from the Family Bank firsthand may have the most familiarity with these principles and the greatest incentive to perpetuate their family's success.

The bank board must also have a close relationship with family members or others that the Family Bank is designed to serve. Regular communication through board meetings and reports can facilitate family members' involvement. While non-trustees would not have power to make decisions at these meetings, their input and attendance should be a requirement to qualify for Family Bank benefits, such as loans.

For smaller estates, one or multiple relatives as trustees can be tasked to conduct the Family Bank's business. Often, several family members can do the job as co-trustees. This may decrease the administrative cost, but it also increases the risk of conflict between heirs and trustees.

The selection of trustees for smaller estates may be *the determining factor* in whether a Family Bank is successful and perpetuated long after the trust grantors are gone. Successor trustees should also be named as much as possible, with language in the trust to allow the designation of others later. If family members can get

Selecting trustees may be the determining factor for your Family Bank's success and perpetuity.

along, family members as trustees can work just fine.

For larger estates, it may be best to have a board of trustees made up of relatives and competent legal and financial professionals who are compensated for their efforts. There will undoubtedly be changes in taxes and regulations that these professionals should help the family navigate. There are a handful of third-party trust administrators familiar with the Family Bank strategy that can do this work for a fee. The larger the amount, the larger the issues that arise with any planning effort; thus, the team that assists may need to be more specialized.

18.
LABORATORIES OF LEARNING

"Experience is the child of Thought, and Thought is the child of Action. We cannot learn men from books."

—Benjamin Disraeli[59]

THE HUMAN BRAIN is a most remarkable organ. Our brains absorb incredible amounts of information every day and then organize, process, and store some of that information. Because of the sheer amount of information our brains must constantly sift through, it's natural that only a minority of important bits will be retained, while whatever is deemed circumstantial or less important will be discarded regularly. You can easily test this phenomenon by trying to remember exactly what family members or coworkers were wearing yesterday or what you had for lunch two or three days ago.

In rare cases, some people are afflicted with a medical condition called *hyperthymesia*[60] that enables them to remember every second of their lives. Many of those with this condition would gladly trade their memory "superpower" for what most of us take for granted: the ability to simply forget the majority of what our senses detect. For the rest of us without perfect memories, unless we have redundant patterns in place or log

---

59 Benjamin Disraeli, *Vivian Grey*, Book 5, Chapter 1 (1826).
60 https://www.bbc.com/future/article/20160125-the-blessing-and-curse-of-the-people-who-never-forget

information somewhere externally, we will automatically forget things; this is not only perfectly normal but is actually preferable.

In the advertising world, regularly forgetting information among all ages is widely accepted as a fact and actually has a name: *the curve of forgetting*.[61] Most of the advertisements you've ever seen or heard were developed to counteract this natural process so that the content is not only easy to remember but sometimes impossible to forget. The proven techniques that advertisers use to mitigate or reverse the curve of forgetting are centered around two principles: emotion and repetition. These two are also easy to test. Can you recall the details of your first automobile accident? How about your first kiss? The strong emotions associated with these events tend to make a long-lasting imprint on the brain. Similarly, you can likely recall nursery rhymes or simple songs like "Twinkle, Twinkle Little Star" with complete accuracy because of the extraordinarily high number of times you've heard or repeated them yourself. Incidentally, music is known in the advertising world as the primary motivator for information retention,[62] but I digress. Applied repetition coupled with positive emotional association has proven to be key to improving our memory besides facilitating better mental health.[63]

A cornerstone responsibility for members of the bank board is to prepare younger members for the world of finance in adulthood. The primary goal of this preparation is to help members remember the principles and practices of the Family Bank through creative and effective methods. Ideally, this training will occur long before members' eighteenth birthdays, but it may occur later as circumstances may necessitate.

As with other legal obligations, these educational

---

61 https://www.avid.org/blog/curve-of-forgetting
62 https://www.frontiersin.org/articles/10.3389/fpsyg.2013.00167/full
63 https://www.apa.org/science/about/psa/2011/03/repetitive-thought and https://www.ncbi.nlm.nih.gov/pmc/articles/PMC2982870/

responsibilities may need to be articulated in legal documents drafted for the establishment of the Family Bank. Bank board members should utilize the same principles of positive emotion and repetition in teaching members sound financial principles. When participants have firsthand, positive experiences observing and engaging in financial transactions, they will be more likely to implement their training and lead more successful lives.

The areas of Bank Board members' responsibility for training younger members on the principles of finance include education, observation, experimentation, and teaching others.

EDUCATION

Perhaps the bank board's most important role is that of educator. The bank board is tasked with ensuring members effectively learn the principles of finance, including savings and investing. This is a crucial responsibility since many families and school systems do not properly prepare young people for the world of finance by the time they reach adulthood. Indeed, one of the first rude awakenings young people face as adults is understanding how long and how much money it will take to pay off student loans, pay off vehicle loans, build up credit, or qualify for a home purchase.

Unfamiliarity with credit cards and other debt obligations can handicap people of all ages as well. I have encountered many individuals who racked up tens of thousands of dollars in high-interest debt by accepting the enticing pitch of "buy now, pay later" and "cash advances." While credit cards and other debt accounts can be useful in certain situations, Americans as a whole pay an enormous amount of unnecessary interest on these accounts every year.

Most parents and teachers try to teach sound financial principles to children, but I have observed that their methods of instruction are mostly ineffective. Positive conversations about money, if they are had at all, are typically rare and brief. Without good examples, the instruction is just theory. Without practice, the theory cannot be proven or disproven by the learner, and thus the theory is more likely to be ignored or forgotten.

Contrast that with members of the Family Bank: they can be introduced to the principles of finance at an early age. Well before reaching an age of responsibility where they have access to capital for schooling, residences, or business undertakings, they have already acquired the skills and habits of good money management from "laboratories of learning" within the Family Bank.

> *Members of the Family Bank are introduced to the principles of finance at an early age.*

The culture inside of families who participate in the Family Bank is supportive and conducive to learning. Rather than money being taboo or the cause of envy or disagreement in a family setting, family members gain familiarity and positive experience when dealing with money. Imagine how empowered young people would feel if they could approach the world of finance with confidence once they reach the age of eighteen. The Family Bank creates an incomparable classroom where one can learn the principles of finance and practice them. This practice or hands-on experimentation is usually the difference between spendthrift heirs and self-made millionaires.

OBSERVATION

The second essential practice in the lab is allowing members to observe real decisions made with real dollars. As I mentioned above, meetings and reports can provide examples, and in-person interaction provides the best opportunities for this learning.

Ideally, after such observation, the member can properly analyze the consequences of specific transactions and draw conclusions. A safe environment, welcoming questions and informed comments, can boost understanding and confidence of the new and young members of the Family Bank.

While I was researching this book, I shared my discoveries with a close friend who is the local store manager of a regional grocer. He recounted an occasion where he witnessed members of the owner's family gather in one of their store's office spaces for a quarterly meeting with members of the executive management team. The current owners had also brought some of their children (aged ten and older) to listen in and participate. My friend was then briefly invited to sit in on the meeting and observe the opening statements.

My friend was intrigued by the collaboration and attention to detail that all the family members had in this joint enterprise, and it was clear that the family had a tradition of holding regular meetings to review their business holdings and teach the next generation the ropes. When more sensitive financial information was ready to be presented, my friend was invited to leave so the family could continue their discussion in private. It was clear to him that this family had a commitment to preserving the family business and the principles that had made them successful, and he was watching something incredibly unique in the business world.

EXPERIMENTATION

The third essential practice in the lab is providing opportunities for members to experiment with money with close supervision. Unlike future loans that will be available in adulthood, subject to contractual terms and interest, these guided activities can permit even minors to participate in financial transactions that may succeed or fail. This is an area where there is significant diversity and adaptation according to each family's preferences. Here, the bank board works with each member for personalized instruction about the family's traditions and opportunities associated with their success. A conscious effort is made to discover members' interests and tailor the training accordingly.

Members should be guided to select several investments or entrepreneurial efforts simultaneously. Like planting a garden or diversifying a portfolio, members need diverse kinds of experiments running at the same time to learn by comparison and contrast. If only one experiment is selected and it fails, the member may become discouraged and give up. It could be more difficult to encourage the member to keep trying. On the other hand, if the one and only experiment succeeds, the member may assume an inappropriate probability of success and experience greater disillusionment the next time he or she fails.

> *Failure isn't tragic; not learning from failure is.*

Failure can be a powerful and unforgettable teacher, and family members and loved ones need room to fail. When asked about his repeated failures as an inventor, Thomas Edison famously quipped, "I have not failed 10,000 times—I've successfully found 10,000 ways that will not work."[64] Failure isn't tragic; not learning from failure is. A wise, experienced guide can assist members to learn from their mistakes and prevent them in the future.

Once the sting of failure is numbed by a number of instructive failures and subsequent successes, members will have greater confidence to assume risk and develop a "nose" for good investments. This introduction to "investing with training wheels" can happen only with specific planning and quite a bit of courage.

One of the youngest examples of this type of supervised

---

64 https://www.smithsonianmag.com/innovation/7-epic-fails-brought-to-you-by-the-genius-mind-of-thomas-edison-180947786/

experimentation I have heard about occurred when two wise parents felt the need to teach their six-year-old daughter, Bonnie, to learn the value of money, savings, and charitable giving. They noticed that most of their family's transactions were digital, and Bonnie wasn't able to observe the budgeting and prioritization of funds that was occurring behind the scenes.

After some mediocre results from helping Bonnie run a few lemonade stands, her parents decided they would have to take a different approach or simply give up. They wanted Bonnie to be excited and involved in the planning and execution of a business enterprise. But how?

Recently, they had received several boxes of children's books donated by some neighboring families whose children had outgrown them. Bonnie was elated. She expressed to her mother her love for books and her desire to be a librarian or bookseller someday. Bonnie's mother wisely paid attention to that comment, and she discussed a plan with Bonnie and the rest of the family to resell some of the nicer, unwanted books in order to make some money. The whole family was excited and got involved in the effort.

They cleaned the books, repaired any damage, and repackaged bundles of books for sale. Since they had capacity for more, they visited a local secondhand store and purchased other books to repair and resell. Soon, they had many bundles of clean, shiny books ready to be sold. Bonnie put the bundles of books together and priced them herself.

Since Bonnie's mother had experience in marketing, she guided her through a series of methods to attract customers. She recommended Bonnie come up with a name for her new business. Bonnie chose the name "Bonnie's Bookshop," and they subsequently contacted a graphic artist to create a logo that was printed on a yard sign, bookmarks, stickers, and invitation cards announcing a sale the following weekend. They went around the neighborhood passing out the invitations. Bonnie's mother even posted information about Bonnie's business and upcoming sale on her social media.

After totaling the purchased books, stationery, and other items, Bonnie's mother tallied approximately forty dollars in expenses. She informed Bonnie of that amount and reminded her that she would need to pay her mother back promptly from her book sales.

The day of the sale arrived and was remarkably successful. Bonnie counted $140 in revenue after they ran out of books and closed shop. Many interested buyers showed up specifically because they were impressed by Bonnie's parents' efforts to teach her sound principles of finance.

After paying back her mother, Bonnie divided the remaining one hundred dollars into separate envelopes labeled "savings," "charity," "spending," and "investing." The last envelope contained designated capital to fund the next book sale, which they did several times with ever-increasing creativity and success.

Recently, Bonnie's mother provided me with an update of Bonnie's latest book sale. Though she had her eye on a new touchscreen tablet, Bonnie felt strongly about dedicating the proceeds of her next sale to purchase school supplies for local refugee families. Weekend sales from Bonnie's Bookstore and other donations totaled $600. Those funds were used to purchase thirty backpacks with school supplies for needy children as well as a stroller for one of the families. What a remarkable example of how to teach these financial principles to young people by helping them *do* activities that help them *live* the principles!

TEACHING OTHERS

The fourth essential practice in the lab is to have members teach the principles they have learned and share their experiences with other members. One of the best ways to remember something is to teach it to someone else. Having personally experienced a few small financial failures and successes in the lab, more experienced members can share their results and perspective with siblings, cousins, or other family and loved ones who are closer in age. I like to think of this practice as comparable to teacher's assistants (TAs) who typically work with college professors. TAs often manage their own classes to assist students not only to better understand the course content but also prepare for exams. TAs may not be as knowledgeable as their sponsoring professor, but they have already been in their students' position and successfully completed the course with distinction.

One of the best ways to remember something is to teach it to someone else.

It may be appropriate to have classroom instruction by a senior member of the bank board followed up by discussions between younger members of the Family Bank moderated by more experienced members. Young people often listen better to their peers than to older instructors, and these "Family Bank TAs" may be tasked to help their counterparts just as they were helped. This effort will not only benefit their peers but will solidify their individual knowledge as well.

Some families adopting the principles and processes of the Family Bank lament that their children and grandchildren are already adults, and it is too late to make use of these laboratories of learning. To this, I respond that I have observed several successful families who created their own Family Bank *after* their children were adults but still funded a variety of different business pursuits run by their adult children and grandchildren. Regardless of age, when individuals gain access to capital linked with responsibility and guidance, they can rapidly learn the principles that will help them become self-sufficient and even wildly successful.

IDEAS FOR IMPLEMENTATION

Below are some financial enterprises I have observed Family Bank members successfully create with assistance and funding from the Family Bank. They are categorized by age.

Young children:

- Secondhand bookstore
- Neighborhood bread and cookie factory
- Egg delivery service
- Teenagers:
- Neighborhood lawn-mowing business
- Snow removal
- Hair products line
- Corn and watermelon sales booths
- Swimming instruction
- Music instruction
- Academic tutoring
- Child care
- Pet care

Adults:

- Real estate sales and development company
- Gun range and dealership

- Online clothing distributor
- Mortgage lender
- Laundromat chain
- Importing business and sales

19.

THE "QUICK-START" FAMILY BANK

"Everything should be made as simple as possible, but not simpler."

—Albert Einstein[65]

HAVE YOU EVER purchased an electronic device or other consumer product and taken a peek at the instruction manual? If so, you may have noticed in the first few pages that there are typically several options for setting up the device. There are often instructions for either a "standard" or a "quick-start" installation process. If you have ever seen those two choices, which of the two have you typically selected?

If you are like most people, you have probably picked the "quick-start" option. Manufacturers are sensitive to their first-time customers' inexperience and make efforts to streamline the installation process with software and automatic defaults. If the name "quick-start" suggests less effort and faster results than the "standard" option, who would not want that, all things being equal? Of course, a "standard" installation may be more appropriate for customers who are more familiar with the product or who have the assistance of an experienced technician. These customers may have more experience navigating the product's customizable features,

---

65 Attributed in *Zanesville Times Recorder*, Zanesville, Ohio, June 22, 1972.

and their individual circumstances may require it.

I have often been asked for instructions on how to establish a "quick-start" Family Bank. As much as the Family Bank's associated principles and practices may make sense, some may not have the resources or expertise to establish a Family Bank in the beginning. Or some may be interested in learning by experimentation on a smaller scale and then expanding from there. Indeed, as we discussed in the last chapter, this type of learning can be the most effective and memorable.

> *The essence of the Family Bank is an idea with plenty of room for adaptation.*

While the Family Banks of certain successful families have a definite legal structure and a set of standardized practices dating back several centuries, the essence of the Family Bank is an idea with plenty of room for adaptation. Indeed, the structure of the Family Bank may morph in time according to regulatory and tax rules. Though the most successful, multigenerational Family Banks have been made up of a series of trusts funded with whole life insurance on the lives of family members, which I will discuss in the next few chapters, a Family Bank can also be started with one hundred dollars in a shoebox. The principles of the Family Bank can be taught regardless of a family's initial cash reserves, and the application of these principles is scalable to fit anyone's means and capabilities.

One could adopt the principles and practices of the Family Bank incrementally as resources permit. In this way, we could compare the development of a Family Bank to the life cycle of a tree. Each phase of development, just like those of a tree, has distinct characteristics.

SEEDLING

Young parents wishing to teach their children the principles of financial management may not have the means to access large sums from their Family Bank. Many in this stage establish individual savings accounts and life insurance policies for each of their children, but it takes time for significant values to accumulate. However, as shown in the chapters, "Compassionate Capitalism" and "Laboratories of Learning," even very small loans can be issued for activities with profit potential.

Young children can quickly learn Family Bank principles if they receive guidance and are given room to experiment. No legal structure, loan contract, or specialized cash reserve account is necessary in these circumstances. Parents can fund loans directly and follow up on the child's efforts themselves. *Note:* young parents wishing to expand their Family Bank *can* and should purchase life insurance policies on children as early as possible for protection and future cash accumulation. We'll explore this in greater detail later.

SAPLING

Those with greater means and experience (as well as older family members) can engage in more sophisticated Family Bank activities and larger loans. The same practices of the "seedling" phase apply here, but with a few added distinctions:

- Sources of funding may come from savings accounts, other accounts, and life insurance policies purchased in the past
- Loan agreements can and should be written and signed

As with the "seedling" phase, a legal structure of trusts or other entities may not be necessary for loans in the "sapling" phase. I have observed approved loans in this phase range from teenagers running seasonal businesses to young adults paying off debts or other expenses. Parents and grandparents made the loans directly to family members with a repayment schedule. Funding can come from a variety of sources. *Note:* parents and grandparents with greater means should regularly allocate funding for their children's and grandchildren's future large expenses, such as schooling, homes, or business creation, into cash equivalent accounts and life insurance.

MATURE TREE

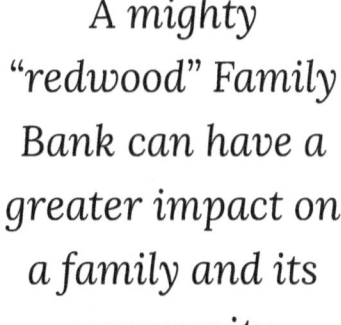

This phase of the Family Bank embraces all the core functions of the Family Bank, including bank board coordination, instruction, sizable loans, grants, and charitable activities. Just as there are many mature trees of different shapes and sizes, not every Family Bank will have the same amounts available to its members for the same purposes.

A mighty "redwood" Family Bank can have a greater impact on a family and its community.

A Family Bank with a cumulative reserve of $100,000 can bless the lives of many family members on a smaller scale. Because of the compounding effect certain cash equivalent accounts and life insurance may have over time, smaller Family Banks may be able to expand their size and capabilities to an increasing number of descendants. But a mighty "redwood" Family Bank with billions of assets, like those of the Rothschilds or Rockefellers, can ostensibly make a greater impact on a family's financial activities and their community.

A final word about individuals—different family members will have different capabilities that could be compared to the same developmental phases. While a young grandson would benefit from a $100 "seedling" loan to help start a lawn-care business, an older aunt may be eligible for a $100,000 loan (or even a loan of millions) to purchase or expand a business. The maximum size of each loan may correspond to a percentage of the Family Bank's total assets or specific accounts funding the loan. Each family will have to individually tailor the size and functions of their Family Bank according to their needs and resources.

20.

FUNDING YOUR BANK: WHERE IS THE MONEY?

"There are three faithful friends: an old wife, an old dog, and ready money."

—Benjamin Franklin[66]

FAMILIES ESTABLISHING FAMILY Banks want to perpetuate their traditions and success easily and for as many generations as possible. Besides establishing trusts or other legal entities for this purpose, they must also incorporate the right kind of "legacy assets" to protect their Family Banks and act as reserves to fund low-interest loans to family members. If the first secret to ensuring family accountability and the continuation of family wealth is loans, then the second secret is having the best loan-funding assets in your Family Bank.

Of all the possible reserve options, cash or cash equivalents provide the most advantages and fewer disadvantages for funding loans from the Family Bank. Since these Family Bank funds need to be ready at a moment's notice, it would be decidedly inconvenient

Cash or cash equivalents are the ideal assets for the Family Bank.

---

66 *Poor Richard's Almanack,* May 1738.

if the assets for funding loans were predominantly locked up in businesses, real estate, or other less liquid assets. Assets that are more liquid but subject to market volatility may also be less than ideal since the market may be down when withdrawals are required.

Of course, the Family Bank does not need to have *all* of its assets in cash or cash equivalents. Owning other, less liquid assets can and should diversify the Family Bank's investments and yield higher returns in support of all its operations. The Family Banks I have observed do not restrict their bank-owned assets to cash or cash equivalents exclusively; some own real estate and other assets that generate a cash flow. When the assets generating income are owned by a trust, families try to offset those earnings by making distributions or charitable donations, a subject explored in detail in a later chapter. Although your Family Bank could very well own many different kinds of assets, an adequate portion of the Family Bank's reserves should be designated for cash or cash equivalents.

The problem with cash is that it usually has a number of disadvantages that could undermine the long-term viability of the Family Bank. Remember that traditional cash accounts are usually available only through banking institutions with several disadvantages, such as low interest that is taxable and limited financial protection. Currency inflation and any applicable taxes have the potential to erase any modest interest gains.

Family Bank boards are aware of these challenges and tend to diversify their assets accordingly. The Family Banks I've seen have had holdings that include real estate, savings accounts, certificates of deposit, money market funds, stocks, and cash-value life insurance.

Wait—cash-value life insurance? It's funny, just mentioning the term "cash-value life insurance" seems to provoke groans from some people. But please hear me out, and permit me to share why some of the wealthiest families in history have chosen to purchase cash-value life insurance.

Besides accomplishing their primary function of protecting individual family members, *properly structured and well-funded* whole life insurance policies can become some of your bank's most valuable assets. This may be the first time you've ever heard anyone refer to a type of life insurance as an asset. True, most kinds of insurance are simply viewed as an expense, a costly safeguard against a variety of risks with even costlier economic consequences. Typically, you won't see any benefit from insurance unless you experience a loss, and insurance is designed to mitigate a loss by providing a means of repairing or replacing that loss. Unfortunately, many permanent life insurance policies are not structured optimally or properly utilized.

Every Family Bank I have observed and researched owns cash-value life insurance, specifically whole life policies, on their members. A few of these banks own as much insurance as the insurance companies will permit them to buy, and policies tend to cover as many family members as possible, from newborns to older family members.

Every Family Bank I've seen owns cash-value life insurance on its members.

Why would the Family Bank own life insurance on its members? There are three important reasons.

Protection—first of all, it's prudent to buy insurance; tragedies like accidents and illness strike nearly every family. Families who establish Family Banks are committed to assisting their members in good times and bad, and life insurance provides unparalleled financial protection against a member's untimely death. Since the economic and emotional loss of a loved one can be devastating, having life insurance on family members owned by the Family Bank can help them recoup and mitigate the costs of a family member's untimely death. The Family Bank can also efficiently assist in the payment of any applicable estate taxes that may be due at the death of its founders. Death-benefit dollars are "discounted" since the policy's death benefit will typically return more tax-free cash than was originally paid into the policy.

Policies purchased on younger family members locks in their insurance eligibility when illness may disqualify them later in life. Many people develop illnesses as they age that may preclude them from purchasing sufficient life insurance, but this problem can be mitigated when the Family Bank purchases a policy on each infant born into the family.

Cash value—many families and business owners also use permanent cash-value life insurance as a tool in their cash-management strategy. Permanent cash-value life insurance policies have a growing cash value that is technically the insurance company's stockpile of cash to fund the future liability of paying the death benefit on the policy. But for ownership purposes, the cash value of a policy is a cash equivalent asset for the owner, whether an individual or other entity. This simultaneous dichotomy of cash reserves for the owner and the insurance company is a very unique arrangement in the financial world. Indeed, this peculiar arrangement creates some remarkable liquidity and tax benefits.

Tax advantages—there are a number of tax considerations that also make life insurance policies an ideal asset for the Family Bank. Structured correctly, the death benefit on such life insurance policies is received income-tax-free. Policies that are owned by trusts may also be structured properly to pay death benefits that are estate-tax-free (see *Crummey v. Commissioner of Internal Revenue*). Whole life policies can grow without income tax, and available loans from cash value can likewise be tax-free. The cash value inside permanent policies grows tax-deferred, and cash values may be received tax-free as long as they don't exceed the policy's basis or are taken as loans. Funds withdrawn from a permanent life insurance policy through loans and withdrawals will reduce the policy's cash value and death benefit.

Believe it or not, some of the largest financial institutions and wealthiest families understand and own permanent cash-value life insurance policies for the death benefit protection *and* the "living benefits" associated with the cash value of those policies. Understanding the living benefits of whole life policies is one of the hardest ideas to "rewire" in people's minds, but it is essential.

Many successful people and businesses use permanent life insurance policies to provide liquidity.

For example, many banks and credit unions allocate part of their reserve holdings or surplus into life insurance when they have an insurable interest and need. Many of the most successful individuals and businesses use the cash values of permanent life insurance policies to provide liquidity when they need it most.

A second idea that is generally stubborn and must be "rewired" in people's minds is that family members may have no ownership of the life insurance policies. Many find it difficult to understand how the "insured," or the life on whom the insurance is written for a whole life policy, may not have any ownership powers. Though heirs must qualify medically for these policies, the Family Bank typically owns and is beneficiary of the policies' values in their entirety. Family members generally have no current or future right to receive any value from the policies unless the Family Bank elects to make a distribution.

The larger the number of individual life insurance policies the Family Bank owns, the greater the chance of its growth and sustainability. Consider the real-world examples of most large corporations: they typically own, pay for, and receive death benefits from insurance policies on their employees in an arrangement known as Corporate-Owned Life Insurance, or COLI. Because of the employer-employee relationship, there is a clear insurable interest in purchasing a policy on the employee. The employee's premature death could bring economic loss to the employer, not to mention creating the cost of finding and training a replacement.

Many large corporations purchase policies on thousands of their employees, and then the law of large numbers comes into play: a certain percentage of employees will die each year, and those multiplied dollars are delivered to the employer. Not only can many of these plans easily become self-funding, but they also provide additional funding for other employee benefits, such as retirement programs and health care. The long-term results of these programs protect the employer and help fund other beneficial efforts.

Perhaps the best real-world example I've heard of implementing this strategy came from the trust officer for a major bank who once told me how he helped an indigenous Alaskan tribe protect itself and generate prosperity for its members several decades ago.

In 1971, President Nixon signed into law one of the largest land claims settlements in US history. The Alaska Native Claims Settlement Act (ANCSA) returned millions of acres of lands to native tribes and villages as well as nearly a billion dollars in compensation for lands seized by the state and federal governments. ANCSA money was distributed through a series of corporations the federal government created that were controlled by the Alaskan villages and tribes. Many of those corporations continue to this day and benefit several hundred federally recognized tribes and villages.

A few years after the law was passed, one Alaskan tribe contacted a major bank for assistance in managing the funds.

The bank forwarded this request to one of its trust officers, and he traveled to the island where the tribe was located to meet with its leadership council. The council members expressed concern with what they were witnessing in some of the other tribes: cash distributions to tribal members were being consumed quickly on travel, new vehicles, and snowmobiles, among other things. The money was not benefiting members of those tribes, as most had expected and hoped.

The tribe's council opened the meeting by listing their goals for the money. First, they wanted the millions of its ANCSA dollars preserved, not wasted. Second, the council expressed an interest in protecting its member families from the financial consequences of untimely deaths of heads of households. The burden of providing for surviving family members had many times fallen on the council, and it was becoming an untenable obligation as the tribe increased in number. Finally, the council wanted some funds to be available to their members for education, home purchases, investments, and business ventures for those who were willing.

The trust officer listened to the council goals and promised to research a solution. He returned a few weeks later with two financial professionals to present their joint proposal. They proposed that life insurance policies written on tribal members could meet all the council's objectives simultaneously. The council would make individual distributions from the ANCSA money to adult members but make them contingent on dedicating a portion to premiums for life insurance policies to be written on each single adult or parent. This program would be voluntary, and the council would retain ownership and control of the policies.

The council agreed to apportion death benefit proceeds to assist survivors with final expenses and income replacement of the deceased. After five years, participants in the program would have access to low-interest loans from the life insurance cash values for activities such as education, home purchases, investments, and even business ventures if the council approved their requests. Each family would have an equal amount available to it, and those found medically ineligible could select another family member as the insured.

When a family member died, part of the death benefit proceeds would be used to purchase policies on surviving family members for the same purposes above. The program would continue perpetually in protecting families and providing low-interest cash to each successive generation.

The tribal council voted affirmatively to adopt the proposal and informed its approximate 1,700 members about the program. Almost every family agreed to participate, and hundreds of whole life policies were purchased through three different mutual life insurance companies on the parents of most families. Implementing the program took several months to complete.

By the time the bank's trust officer retired several years later, a number of tribal members had already passed away, and their surviving family members were greatly comforted by the insurance benefit. He noted how each family followed the program and consented for the tribe to purchase additional policies on other family members to make the program available to them as well. The program has been remarkably successful and continues to this day.

This example represents one of the more successful applications of Family Bank principles I have heard to date. The former trust officer who shared the report was amazed at the program's success in a noticeably brief time. Wise counsel from an advisor with access to the tools for implementation has already benefited several generations of this tribe.

21.

DESIGNING YOUR IDEAL LEGACY ASSETS

*"Money isn't everything . . .
but it ranks up there with oxygen."*

—Rita Davenport[67]

SINCE THE OLDEST and largest Family Banks have been continuously purchasing whole life insurance on their family members generation after generation, many learning about the Family Bank want to know why. Whole life insurance is less common and less well-known than the cash and cash-equivalent accounts often owned by the Family Bank, and people usually need more information about it to understand its important role in the Family Bank. Whole life insurance has some characteristics that actually make it fundamental to the Family Bank, for reasons I'll detail in this chapter.

Of all the types of life insurance, whole life is the oldest, and a form of whole life insurance has been around since the Middle Ages.[68] The name *whole life* comes from the fact that the policy is designed to remain in force throughout an insured's entire life

---

67   Rita Davenport and John David Mann, *Funny Side Up: A Southern Girl's Guide to Love, Laughter, and Money* (Cape May, NJ: Success Publishers, 2012).
68   https://www.jstor.org/stable/1011003?seq=1#page_scan_tab_contents

and beyond life expectancy. It is a remarkably simple product compared to many other types of life insurance.

Whole life insurance is a contract where the owner agrees to pay a guaranteed level premium, and the insurance company guarantees a level death benefit payable to the designated beneficiaries whenever the insured passes away. The premium corresponds with the amount of the death benefit and the age and health rating of the insured(s). All things being equal, the younger and healthier the individual, the lower the premium usually is. In most cases, the death benefit is generally received income-tax-free.

Inside a whole life insurance policy is a growing cash value just like in other permanent cash-value life insurance policies. What is the purpose of this cash value? Technically, it's the insurance company's stockple of cash to fund the future liability of a death benefit. The cash value of a whole life insurance policy is guaranteed to increase incrementally and is designed to equal the death benefit at a certain age, typically age 100. Note that all guarantees are backed by the claims-paying ability of the issuing insurance company.

Dividends paid into whole life policies from mutual companies can increase the death benefit and cash value.

In addition to the guaranteed cash increase, most whole life policies offered by mutual companies are eligible for dividends that increase the death benefit and cash value. Dividends typically come from companies' profits and are not guaranteed. Financially-stronger companies tend to have better historical dividend records. And because dividends are somewhat correlated to prevailing interest rates, the dividend can act as a sort of inflation protection for the policy's cash value.

Term insurance is a popular form of life insurance, particularly among young people, and most of us own some type of term insurance at some point in our lives. Term insurance is pure death benefit: you pay the premium, and the company pays a death benefit. There generally is no residual value or other benefits. The word *term* refers to a temporary time frame such as ten, twenty, or thirty years in which the premiums and death benefit stay level. Beyond that time frame, the premiums for most policies increase annually at a high rate. The scale mirrors mortality tables for life expectancy, and they look like a *J* on a graph, increasingly trending upward. That upward trend is due to an increased risk of death with the increase in age. Insurance company actuaries must account for that increased risk; therefore, the companies charge a much higher premium at older ages.

In sum, term insurance is generally a short-term solution but can get more and more expensive if you keep paying the increasing premiums. If policy owners continue to pay the increasing term premiums up to life expectancy, they will likely pay more in cumulative premiums than will be received as a death benefit. Unless family members are consistently dying young, this kind of life insurance will not work in a Family Bank framework.

There are other kinds of permanent life insurance that could potentially work in a Family Bank. Unfortunately, these are all based on an insurance model developed in the 1980s called "universal life" that has some prohibitive disadvantages. Universal life, or UL, has an increasing cost of insurance identical to a term policy but has a cash value that can grow by a minimum interest rate (fixed universal life, or FUL), market returns with a variable universal life (VUL) tied to investment sub-accounts, or a kind of hybrid of the two, indexed universal life (IUL).

While the several types of universal life insurance may offer

> *The rising costs and uncertain returns of other types of cash-value life insurance make them a less reliable asset for the Family Bank."*

more attractive growth in hypothetical projections than whole life—and while they could possibly deliver higher cash value in the future—their rising costs and uncertain return make them a less reliable asset for the Family Bank. These policies also lack the internal guarantees of whole life policies that can be essential to the Family Bank's long-term viability.

Since the Family Bank is not purchasing life insurance policies on family members primarily for the cash growth anyway, for most people, a conservative but competitive return will do. Avoiding the frustration of down markets and increasing costs of insurance can simplify things considerably. The real money to be made is for the family members and loved ones who research investments, work hard, have access to capital to fund their endeavors, and then enjoy the fruits of those efforts.

What kind of whole life policies should the Family Bank own? There are three keys to making whole life insurance on yourself, relatives, and loved ones an asset worthy of your Family Bank.

1. The company—not all insurance companies are created equal. There is an old saying in our industry that "There is no such thing as guarantees, only *guarantors*." An insurance company's promise is only as strong as its ability to pay. Policies with a financially superior, "mutual" insurance company paying dividends work best. *Mutual* refers to the ownership of an insurance company; unlike publicly traded companies, mutual companies do not have

shareholders. Instead, they are stockless and operate for the benefit of current and future policyowners.

Mutual insurers have the right business structure to offer competitive whole life contracts with dividends. Owners of a "participating policy" from a mutual insurer act like stockholders with voting rights and receive dividend payments when they are declared. Since mutual companies do not have to answer to Wall Street, they make decisions based on a long-term perspective and don't follow short-term trends. Their interests are better aligned with those of their policyowners who seek financial security and guaranteed growth.

2. The type—not all whole life policies are created equal either. Some companies may "penalize" you if you loan funds from the policy. This practice is known as *direct recognition*, and companies practicing it will adjust their annual dividend to an individual whole life policy proportionately to whatever policy loan against the policy's cash value is outstanding. Besides direct recognition, many products from the different companies have different premiums, guarantees, risk classes, mortality experiences, company expenses, policy loan rates, interest rates, and dividend history. With many factors to consider, it is prudent to investigate all the details before committing to buy one policy over another.

3. The structure—this is the secret to making whole life policies perform like valuable assets, and this is where you need the right agent to help you. Properly structured policies are designed to reduce the commissions and costs on the policy while optimizing the death benefit and cash accumulation. A typical policy will have a proportionately lower whole life "face amount" with a low-cost term

insurance rider that allows extra cash to be deposited.

The Internal Revenue Service has guidelines for how much money can fund life insurance policies based on the total insurance amount and age, and not following those rules can have adverse tax consequences on the cash value of the policy. (See Modified Endowment Contract [MEC] rules.) Adding term insurance riders can help clients stay within those limits while adding additional cash and making the policy more efficient than a traditionally structured whole life policy. *Note*: many companies have contractual limits on adding additional cash that must be considered besides policy MEC limits.

Even if a policy is structured optimally, there is typically a delay in accumulating significant cash inside of policies for several years. Withdrawals of substantial amounts of cash for large purchases can usually occur only many years after the policy was started and generously funded, and many people simply do not have the time and money to make it work for them. The Family Bank can synthesize the functions of a personal bank with a family legacy bank: individuals with disposable income can make use of properly structured whole life contracts to benefit themselves as well as younger family members and loved ones with fewer financial resources.

Couples old and young can often help accomplish their planning goals by purchasing joint "second to die" or "survivorship" policies. These policies are designed to pay a death benefit after the second insured dies, and the internal costs tend to be lower than individual policies since two lives are underwritten. The cash value of these policies also tends to grow competitively.

Often, the best time to purchase a policy on children or grandchildren is when they are young. But there are advantages and disadvantages to purchasing

The Family Bank
purchases policies

these policies at any age. Because the premium on the policy is partially based on age, a policy on a younger person will have a lower insurance cost because that young person has a lower probability of death. However, larger premiums on a young person tend to disproportionately increase the death benefit for the same reason: higher premiums can boost the death benefit significantly. The cash value of the policy also typically takes longer to compound inside a policy on a younger person than an older person. To stay within MEC limits, a larger amount of death benefit will be required for the first seven years. This can be achieved with a lower-cost term rider added to the base whole life policy. This strategy mirrors what the Rockefellers and other wealthy families have done once a new relative is born into the family.

22.

IMPLEMENTING THE BUSINESS OF FAMILY BANKING

"Business? It's quite simple. It's other people's money.[69]*"*

—Alexandre Dumas Jr.

AT THE HEART of operations within the Family Bank is the primary tool of improving the lives of its members: low-interest loans. I have heard people refer to this tool as "the great secret" or the "grand key" to ensuring family accountability and the perpetuation of family wealth. I like to refer to it as the only way you can give your loved ones *all* the benefits of wealth without giving them a penny; but how is that possible? How can you give someone nothing and everything simultaneously?

> *Low-interest loans are the "grand key" of the Family Bank.*

Around 1810, near the end of his life, Mayer Amschel Rothschild sought to facilitate his children's financial independence and further expand their family's successful banking business internationally. He drew up a partnership agreement and installed his five sons in the five major banking hubs of Europe at the time: Frankfurt, London, Naples, Paris, and Vienna. Each son had sole

---

[69] *La Question d'Argent*, Act 2, Scene 7 (1857).

responsibility and control over his respective bank, and each was required to join the others in meeting regularly to exchange information about the economic and political trends in each geographic region. This network of constant information opened up tremendous financial opportunities for the family throughout Europe that continues to this day.

To fund the creation of each son's bank, Mayer did something unique then and now: he did not *give* his sons a penny to start their banks. Instead, he *loaned* it to them.[70] Each son was expected to repay his loan with interest, and the loans codified their father's expectation of productivity and efficiency from his sons. The loans' accruing interest motivated each son to repay the loans quickly and helped spur them to enormous success.

Each successive generation of Rothschilds continued to loan, not give, each other money for a variety of purposes in the same pattern.[71] The message from this example is clear: if you would like to see your children and subsequent generations achieve great financial success, then the secret may be to *not* give them anything.

The secret to giving your family everything may be to give them nothing.

But should one really just ignore his or her descendants' needs and capabilities and not offer them anything? Of course not. Mayer Rothschild did not hoard his wealth nor abandon his family responsibilities. Instead, he was actively engaged with them, training them, and investing directly in their financial activities. Later, the family ultimately built a financial empire that grew to one of the largest private family fortunes in history.

---

70   David R. York and Andrew L. Howell, *Entrusted: Building a Legacy that Lasts* (YH Publishing, LLC, 2015), 187–190.
71   Ibid.

Mayer laid the foundation for this feat in part by initially offering opportunities with accountability: low-interest loans to be repaid by his children. Mayer's sons followed his lead by taking advantage of the unparalleled opportunities their father provided by making his substantial wealth available to them in the right way.

How exactly does the Family Bank make loans to its members? Previously, we have discussed the advantages of a trust owning and controlling cash-equivalent assets that are managed by trustees. The process trustees follow to make those cash assets available to family members through loans can be as simple or as complex as the family wishes. The trustees or board of trustees can make up the Family Bank board for lending purposes, and here are some typical steps they would take to offer low-interest loans to family members:

- An invitation—the bank board invites adults in the family or group to receive low-interest loans for qualified activities if they so choose. The trust language may spell out those specific activities, or the board may have more discretion. Acceptable activities may relate directly to improving the member's financial situation and may include funding for education, home purchases, business funding, real estate investments, or charitable activities, to name a few.

- A proposal—members wishing to receive funding meet with the board and discuss the new enterprise. Funding may depend on the activity's potential for increasing asset value or earning income from the activity. First loans may be smaller for less experienced or younger members.

- A vote—the board weighs the applicant's training, history, and capabilities. The viability and potential success of the endeavor is judged and voted on. The approved loan amount may change from applicant to applicant.

- A contract—if the proposal is approved, the board draws up terms for a loan along with a repayment schedule. Collateral may or may not be necessary (see contingencies below). Depending on the activity, the duration of the loan could be short or extend to multiple decades. The interest factor minimum may follow the Internal Revenue Service "Applicable Federal Rates" regarding private-party loans.

- A mentor—the member is assigned to report failures or successes regularly to a member of the board or one of his or her assistants. The mentor may also provide guidance.

- Funding—cash is drawn from cash accounts or loans from the cash value of whole life insurance policies.

- Payments—regular repayments from the member are credited back to repay the whole life insurance policy loans. Any applicable interest from repayments may be offset by distributions or charitable donations if applicable.

- A pattern—after the applicant has a proven record of competence and success, larger loans may be available in the future.

CONTINGENCIES

Inevitably, some members may not be able to fulfill their loan-agreement contract for a variety of reasons. Another question I hear nearly every time I present this concept is "What if the member falls behind or defaults on the loan?"

One of the great advantages of holding the cash reserves for family loans within whole life insurance is the ability to cover multiple contingencies that may arise, such as the following:

- Death—often, a member's maximum loan amount may not exceed the insurance benefit on his or her life, and life insurance on the member may repay any outstanding loan in case of death. Death benefits of policies on family members will also bring additional assets to the bank that can be reinvested into new policies on younger family members (as long as there is an insurable interest that is subject to underwriting requirements).

- Disability—since disability from an accident or illness is something we could all face, and since it could affect Family Bank loan recipients' ability to repay their loans, families with Family Banks should consider ways to guard against that risk. It's prudent to review whole life policy features to see if standard or supplemental protections are available. Such product protections are worth careful consideration when purchasing permanent life insurance inside the Family Bank.

- Defaults—if the member fails to make repayments, the board may bar the member from any future benefits or loans. Loan forgiveness may occur on a case-by-case basis, and a probationary period may apply before the next loan. An inevitable death benefit can eventually replenish the lost funds, potentially avoiding the need for litigation or repossession. Note that forgiven loans may have tax consequences.

One of the best examples I know of whole life policies providing a lifetime of opportunities with accountability comes from a long-time client who had recently celebrated the birth of a new grandson. He contacted our office and expressed a desire to help his grandson with college and other important milestones in life. We initially showed him a joint-income annuity with an annual payment that would continue throughout the grandson's life, but our client was not thrilled about dedicating a considerable sum of cash to generate an annual cash handout with little or no accountability for his grandson. In addition, the grandson may need access to lump sums of funding for certain purchases that may not be available through a steady income stream.

Upon further research, we suggested using a whole life policy to help accomplish his goals. The results since then have been remarkable. In the future, the policy could help provide funds for major life events, such as education, a home purchase, a business purchase, investment funding, and retirement income. Even though this loving grandfather may not be around to witness those life events, his wise planning and asset positioning of a whole life policy can help make them more feasible.

> *Wise grandparents can help their grandchildren from beyond the grave.*

Even though the Family Bank may not necessarily be a lifelong lender to its members—and, ideally, members who successfully practice the principles of investing and management will be able to self-fund investments in the future—the Family Bank can give them a crucial start on the path to financial independence and prosperity at crucial financial crossroads in life.

23.
HOW MUCH IS ENOUGH?

"'Don't put all your eggs in one basket' is all wrong. I tell you, 'put all your eggs in one basket, and then watch that basket.'"

—Andrew Carnegie[72]

AFTER UNDERTAKING THE creation of their Family Bank, many of my clients have asked, "How much of my estate should be allocated to our Family Bank?" A bold but accurate response could be this: "Only allocate whatever amount you don't want to be wasted." Exactly how much money is given to heirs and how much is set aside for loans from the Family Bank will be different for each family. Warren Buffett offers advice in this area: "You should leave your children enough so they can do anything, but not enough so they can do nothing."[73] Selecting the amount of gifted wealth is a personal decision that families will have to make depending on the wishes of the older generation and the circumstances of their descendants. But there is little doubt that whatever money is given is more likely to be consumed. Money dedicated to the Family Bank, on the other hand, has the potential to grow and provide benefits to the family.

Whole life insurance can ensure the generational growth of

---

[72] Address to students at Curry Commercial College, Pittsburg, PA, June 23, 1885.
[73] https://www.forbes.com/sites/angelauyeung/2018/06/01/warren-buffetts-advice-on-how-to-raise-well-adjusted-heirs/?sh=6bbe2a47712f

the Family Bank's assets. Insurance is a cash multiplier by design. An interesting phenomenon can occur when properly structured whole life insurance is part of the Family Bank: that portion of the bank's portfolio could eclipse the bank's other assets in time. This can certainly be true if an economic crisis depresses other assets such as real estate inside the Family Bank's portfolio. But even in good times, the multiplier function of the insurance can deliver income-tax-free returns.

Insurance is a multiplier by design.

One analogy demonstrating life insurance's long-term potential comes from the farm: think of a small-time farmer who loads his wheat harvest onto an oversized truck. If he sells the entire load, his wheat will be ground into flour and provide sustenance for hundreds of people. But that is the end of his crop's benefit since none was retained for future planting.

To prepare seeds for the following year, many farmers designate a portion of their acreage to "seed" wheat. *Seed wheat* is just what it sounds like; it is harvested and saved for seeding the next year's crop. It usually comes from the best acreage and receives the extra protection of pesticides and fungicides. Because each head of wheat contains about thirty kernels and one pound of wheat contains approximately 15,000 kernels, it doesn't take very much acreage to seed thousands of acres. In 2019, one acre of farm ground in the United States yielded on average fifty-two bushels of harvested wheat, but it only took about one bushel to seed it.[74] A thousand acres of wheat could be seeded with less than twenty acres of seed.[75] Similarly, a small portion of an estate dedicated to the Family Bank and funded by life insurance can yield significantly higher values in the future.

---

74 https://www.nass.usda.gov/Publications/Todays_Reports/reports/cropan20.pdf
75 Ibid.

The last example I like to use comes from my own family's experience with a sourdough starter. Sourdough yeast is a single-celled organism that belongs to the kingdom of fungi. It feeds on carbohydrates and releases carbon dioxide and alcohol as byproducts in a process called *fermentation*. Without yeast, alcoholic beverages would not exist, and many baked goods would be hard and dense. Yeasts come in several varieties with distinct characteristics and uses.

The baking yeast in the grocery store is a relatively new product. Ancient Egyptian bakers were the first to extensively use yeast or "leaven" in their baked goods. They discovered that certain batches of dough left alone for a few hours would naturally fluff up while others would remain flat and dense. The source of their leaven could have been yeast spores in the air or spores that were growing on the milled flour itself. Once leaven was identified, bakers removed a small portion of their fluffy dough and saved it for the next batch. Like clockwork (or sundials in this case), a starter was added to a new batch and fluffed everything up with carbon dioxide after a few hours. The bakers repeated the process with each successive batch, constantly removing and adding starters in a cycle.

Many sourdough yeasts have been recycled and handed down for generations. My family has a starter that has been in our family for about fifty years, and we were given the starter by another family that passed it down for more than two hundred years. We were told that our particular starter came from Basque sheepherders between Spain and France and that they cradled it close on cold nights to keep it warm and alive. Researchers at the University of Utah have even evaluated our starter, and they have confirmed that a number of other bacteria are thriving along with the sourdough yeast, accomplishing the same task of flavoring and leavening the batter.

Because the sourdough yeast is a living organism, it must be nurtured and protected to live and grow. All organisms create waste products, and these are often lethal to the organism. After several days and weeks, a sourdough starter will create a clear, alcoholic fluid on the top of the receptacle. Unless the starter is regularly used and replenished, it will eventually die from its own waste products. Thus, a healthy starter is one that is used on a regular basis.

What does any of this have to do with money? Well, sourdough starters can serve as a powerful analogy to describe how best to protect and grow money. Like yeast, money can magnify and multiply things. A little can create an enormous difference over time. Imagine that a family's wealth is akin to a large batch of sourdough batter. If the batch is consumed in the form of gifts to children or charity at the death of the parents, it can be lost forever. But if a portion of that wealth is off-limits to consumption by heirs, it can be grown in future batches. Family members could receive their own "starter" or loan from the Family Bank and create their own batches of sourdough goods. If the batches are grown and recycled in the proper manner, they can be the source of increased wealth and charitable donations for generations to come.

> *A little can make a significant difference.*

24.
CHARITABLE CONSIDERATIONS

"Surplus wealth is a sacred trust which its possessor is bound to administer in his lifetime for the good of the community."

—Andrew Carnegie[76]

YEAR AFTER YEAR, Americans lead the world in charitable giving to the tune of hundreds of billions of dollars.[77] We also hover at the top of countries in the world donating volunteer hours, helping strangers, and efficiently providing aid to the needy in every corner of the globe. The hand of providence seems to smile warmly on this nation, and we individually and collectively demonstrate our gratitude by opening our wallets and volunteering our time.

Many millionaire and billionaire families are among the greatest donors to charitable causes. Among others, the Rockefeller family has a tradition of directly involving family members with the selection and benefit of worthy causes. John Rockefeller Jr. said that philanthropy ought to be at the center of the family's financial activities—"For every right implies a responsibility; every opportunity, an obligation; every possession, a duty."[78] It has been

---

76 Andrew Carnegie, "The Gospel of Wealth," *North American Review,* June 1889; https://www.carnegie.org/about/our-history/gospelofwealth/

77 https://home.treasury.gov/news/press-releases/sm1040

78 https://www.cnbc.com/2018/03/26/david-rockefeller-jr-shares-4-secrets-to-wealth-and-family.html

reported that the Rockefeller family regularly donates $50 million every year to charitable causes.[79]

Charitable giving is a beautiful expression of generosity that benefits millions of needy recipients who would otherwise suffer from disease, malnutrition, or other difficulties. Many estate plans outline future philanthropic efforts and disbursements set up by charitably-minded people. Often, these plans simultaneously satisfy estate tax obligations or other personal reasons as we discussed earlier. Sometimes personal reasons for charitable giving can stem from a sense that children and others have already received sufficient gifts and sometimes from a lack of confidence in the financial capabilities of one's heirs. Regardless of the reasons, charities welcome donations and proactively court the attention of possible wealthy benefactors.

There is an important aspect of charities that all donors should keep in mind: they are run by people. Because of that human element, they can be susceptible to the same consumptive and even entitled practices when they receive a windfall of cash. Many charitable organizations have been dubiously featured in news articles after it was disclosed that management directed no more than a single-digit percentage of donations to worthy causes.[80] The bulk of donations in those cases were spent on administrative costs and fundraising. Some organizations have paid millions in annual compensation to their presidents/CEOs, with the highest-paid executive receiving more than five million dollars in 2019.[81]

Every charity has an inherent flaw: they are run by people.

---

79 https://www.rockefellerfoundation.org/news/the-rockefeller-foundation-commits-50-million-in-funding-for-global-coronavirus-response-in-2020-annual-letter-covid-19-meeting-this-moment/
80 https://www.consumerreports.org/charities/best-charities-for-your-donations-a4066579102/
81 https://www.charitywatch.org/top-charity-salaries

The daughter of one of our wealthy clients once recounted an experience of visiting the headquarters of a local charitable nonprofit that her family's foundation had benefitted for many years. When she arrived in the parking lot, she noted three brand-new, high-end luxury vehicles parked in the spots reserved for the executive team. During their visit, she casually asked about the new vehicles parked outside. The CEO of the charity was pleased to report that they were a reward for their top three fundraisers for meeting their fundraising goals. Our client's daughter finished the meeting and reported her observation to the family: "I went back and suggested that the charity didn't need our donation that year," she said.

Most of the charities that my clients have chosen to benefit have enjoyed a proven track record of efficiently delivering aid to the needy. Many churches and religious charities enjoy this distinction, though the details of their expenditures and the compensation of their management may not be publicly disclosed.[82]

If charities could best manage money, why would they keep asking for donations?

Even when charities are efficient in their investments and distributed aid, they are ostensibly designed to transfer financial resources rather than to grow them. When the Red Cross delivers the equivalent of millions of dollars in meals and water bottles to victims of hurricanes, for example, those millions are consumed and gone forever. Some large charities and nonprofits have massive endowments to fund their activities, but there are strict rules regulating the investment options and minimum annual spending requirements. Those who manage charitable

---

[82] https://www.charitywatch.org/resources-for-donors#warning-to-donors

endowments also may not be the most proficient since Wall Street has a way of poaching top talent through more competitive compensation. And if charities were particularly adept at managing and growing wealth themselves, why would they keep asking for and accepting donations every year?

Many wealthy families seek to bypass the administrative "baggage" and expense of established charities by creating their own family foundations. Many appoint heirs to the board or management team of these foundations. It is important to note that there are some burdensome regulations and tax laws associated with foundations, and outside legal and tax advice are usually required to ensure that their operations are in compliance with all applicable laws and regulations. One big disadvantage to foundations is their restriction from directly benefitting or loaning funds to family members or loved ones who are considered "disqualified persons."[83] A common goal of foundations, on the contrary, is sometimes to give heirs the opportunity and responsibility to use the family's wealth to help others *outside* the family.

Family foundations can be complicated.

When asked about establishing a charitable foundation with his family's wealth, Prince Harry, Duke of Sussex, responded,

> I think at the moment, my wife and I, we were being directed toward starting a foundation but we actually decided there is [sic] probably enough foundations out there doing amazing work. . . . And there's a hell of a lot of money being passed around the world and there are so many problems but we thought we'd just take a moment and see if there was some form of other organization or different entity we could create that could bring people

---

83 https://www.irs.gov/charities-non-profits/private-foundations/loans

together, rather than us just starting a foundation. We don't think the world needs necessarily another foundation from us.[84]

Other families have felt the same way. The rules on foundations are cumbersome, and foundations may not be their best choice. But what is a better way for a family to engage in charitable activities? How can a family best benefit their family and the community simultaneously?

A friend of mine once found the answer in a remarkable way and told me the story of his family's donation to their church. The church was preparing to begin a large construction project, and many private donors offered to pay the costs of the project. My friend and his relatives offered a significant donation, and they were invited to meet in person with the project's director to deliver the check. In the director's private office, my friend handed him the check and said, "We're happy to give more, if it's needed."

"We would rather have more donors than donations."

The director looked at him and at the check and smiled. He responded with something like this: "This is a common experience for us. There are so many generous church members offering donations, and it is often more than we need. If we accept more from you at this time, we will have to go hire some recent college graduates and task them with investing the money to grow it. But obviously you and your family know how to grow it just fine. If we need more, we will let you know. But why don't you keep those funds and use them to teach all your family how to make money the way you have? We would rather have more donors than donations."

---

84 https://www.foxnews.com/entertainment/harry-reportedly-reveals-agony-over-megxit-in-call-to-hoaxers-posing-as-greta-thunberg

My friend said this conversation opened his eyes to the true nature of his and his family's financial stewardship. He had never considered that charities would and *should* prefer regular, smaller donations rather than large one-time gifts, especially since receiving ongoing donations is easier than managing large endowment funds. Most importantly, the habitual sacrifice of making regular donations for good causes graces individuals with an increased sense of humility and gratitude. Providence often smiles on those who selflessly serve others.

Those inclined to make large gifts can certainly do so, and very wealthy families may have little choice if the alternative is remitting large sums to the Internal Revenue Service. But I like to suggest an alternative to large gifts to charitable people by presenting the following.

"What is better: donate a one-time sum of $10 million today, or donate tens of millions over the lifespan of your descendants?" Money, potentially growing perpetually, can accomplish this feat.

If charities are susceptible to the same entitled or wasteful behavior that people can be, donating funds on an ongoing basis instead of donating one-time or occasional large gifts may be a better way of ensuring the charity's accountability. Those who choose this option can still empower the children to collaborate every year and decide which charities are most deserving of distributions from the Family Bank. Growing money provides this opportunity, and constantly growing cash values in whole life insurance policies held within the Family Bank can help accomplish this goal.

> **Regular donations rather than one-time gifts can help keep charities accountable.**

25.
WEATHERING FINANCIAL CRISES

"I define a recession as when your neighbor loses his job, but a depression is when you lose your own."

—Dave Beck[85]

YOU AND OTHERS may see trouble coming in the financial world. Monetary and geopolitical forces could have a long-term negative impact on your family and loved ones. How can you protect what you have built as well as those you care for?

Everyone goes through tough financial situations at some point in life. The consequences of these crises reverberate more broadly within a family as multiple family members may be directly and negatively affected. I have seen contention, envy, and despair arise between siblings and parents when one goes through a financial crisis.

Cash in a crisis can be the difference between survival and ruin.

Financial strain can rip marriages and relationships apart as quickly as anything. The solution to such crises is to plan and prepare by having financial resources available to depend on during the lean times. Cash or cash equivalents tend to be what people and businesses need to keep their

---

85 Dave Beck, quoted in *Time*, February 22, 1954; cited in Fred R. Shapiro, ed., *The Yale Book of Quotations* (New Haven, CT: Yale University Press, 2006), 49.

doors open and food on the table. But the problem is that most businesses and families trying to make ends meet do not keep a sufficient cash reserve to weather financial crises.

Desperation in the face of personal or widespread financial crises obliges many to borrow money to meet their financial obligations. In those situations, Americans often rely on credit cards that typically have higher-than-average interest rates associated with any outstanding balances. Others without savings or credit resources must sell property or assets—likely at a discount—to quickly acquire the funds. Finally, some must rely on the generosity of others through charity or government assistance. All these sources of assistance present a variety of disadvantages to those who are forced to seek them.

During the Great Depression years of 1930 to 1933, it is estimated that more than 9,000 banks failed, more than one-third of all the banks in the nation.[86] In contrast, only 20 of a total of 350 insurance companies went into receivership during the same time period, and only about 1 percent of all in-force insurance policies were implicated.[87] Part of this was due to the stricter state regulations regarding investment choices and reserves (liquidity) that insurance companies must maintain as opposed to other financial institutions. Few states permitted insurers to invest in the stock market at the time, and those companies had no direct exposure to the 1929 stock market crash.[88] Notwithstanding the struggles of some insurance companies, other solvent companies "reinsured" the insolvent insurers and virtually all claims were still honored.[89] Some insurance companies actually *prospered*[90] during the Great

---

86   https://www.fdic.gov/exhibit/p1.html#/10
87   http://www.bested.com/studyguides/NMIL-IUS/NMIL-IUS.pdf
88   https://www.referenceforbusiness.com/history2/64/New-York-Life-Insurance-Company.html
89   https://www.naic.org/documents/cipr_home_130823_implications_industry_trends_final.pdf
90   https://www.history.com/news/great-depression-people-who-made-money

Depression as many Americans recognized the need to shore up their finances in case of an accident or the premature death of a loved one.

> *The Family Bank can assist your family members when others will not or cannot.*

Imagine if people never had to rely on the government, banks, credit cards, charities, or churches for support if their financial world came screeching to a halt. Imagine how much less consumer and governmental debt there would be and how much more economic prosperity could take its place. What if, in an act of remarkable selflessness, your great-grandparents had earmarked part of their fortune to remain accessible to their descendants for the inevitable tough times that would come? Wouldn't that create a memorable and worthwhile legacy?

It has been said that history doesn't repeat itself, but it does rhyme. Families and others have the opportunity now to help protect their own from financial catastrophes all while helping to ensure accountability. Cash resources from the Family Bank can be the best source of this assistance when the next disaster strikes.

26.
AN INCREASING NEED FOR FAMILY FINANCING

"If you think education is expensive—try ignorance."

—Derek C. Bok[91]

THE WORLD WE live in today is a complicated place, and things seem to be getting more complicated and expensive every year. Our daily activities often revolve around technology and conveniences that were unthinkable a few hundred years ago, or even a few decades ago. With the advancement and increased complexity of products and services come greater costs. Many of the large expenses that are considered essential in society today carry a price tag far greater than the same necessities only a few decades ago.

Consider the increased cost of the traditional automobile from a generation ago. The average new vehicle in 1970 cost approximately $3,542.[92] The median household income that year was $9,870,[93] and a new vehicle represented *36 percent* of median household earnings. Contrast that percentage with the average cost

---

91 Attributed in Paul Dickson, *The Official Rules* (New York: Dell Publishing, 1978).
92 https://www.chicagotribune.com/news/ct-xpm-1996-06-16-9606160132-story.html
93 https://www.census.gov/library/publications/1971/demo/p60-78.html#:~:text=The%20median%20money%20income%20of,the%201969%20figure%20of%20%249%2C430

of a vehicle in 2020 at $38,961,[94] *58 percent* of $67,521, the median household income in that year.[95] The regulatory requirements of federal CAFE standards,[96] technological advances and standard conveniences, and the rising cost of materials of modern automobiles has caused the price of everyday transportation to nearly *double* what it once was.

Another mainstay of everyday living in the United States is the single-family residential home. The price of the median US home fifty years ago in the fourth quarter of 1970 was $22,600,[97] or $159,000 today, adjusted for inflation.[98] By the fourth quarter of 2020, the median price of a single-family home reached $358,700,[99] more than 2.25 times higher than the price of homes fifty years ago. The rising costs of conventional homes may be part of the reason so many Americans are unable to afford home ownership and why younger Americans in particular are seeking alternatives.[100]

Another traditional expense that has ballooned in cost over the past decades is college education. As modern life has become more complex and expensive, more students have been obliged to seek higher education to improve their earning potential. Unfortunately, the costs of higher education have risen faster than wages,[101] and the average cost of a four-year college degree per year

---

94 https://www.consumerreports.org/buying-a-car/people-spending-more-on-new-cars-but-prices-not-necessarily-rising-a3134608893/
95 https://www.census.gov/library/publications/2021/demo/p60-273.html#:~:text=Median%20household%20income%20was%20%2467%2C521,median%20household%20income%20since%202011.
96 https://www.nhtsa.gov/laws-regulations/corporate-average-fuel-econom
97 https://fred.stlouisfed.org/series/MSPUS
98 https://www.bls.gov/data/inflation_calculator.htm
99 https://fred.stlouisfed.org/series/MSPUS
100 https://www.attomdata.com/news/market-trends/home-sales-prices/attom-data-solutions-q4-2020-u-s-home-affordability-report/
101 https://www.forbes.com/sites/camilomaldonado/2018/07/24/price-of-college-increasing-almost-8-times-faster-than-wages/?sh=6b83536566c1

including room, board, and other fees reached $28,775[102] per year in 2020, totaling $115,100 for the entire experience. Adjusting for inflation, the average four-year degree from a public university is almost 2.5 times what it was fifty years prior.[103] With higher education costs increasing, it's no wonder many Americans are struggling to repay student loans and are seeking relief.

With these major expenses and many others increasing in cost, many Americans are finding difficulty making these purchases without incurring a disproportionately large amount of debt. The staggering costs of education and homes are beginning to exceed the financial eligibility of borrowers. For example, because the median monthly cost of home ownership exceeded lenders' benchmark debt-to-income[104] ratio in 2020, borrowers may soon find themselves unable to qualify for traditional mortgages if this unprecedented phenomenon continues. Borrowers may be obliged to seek higher-interest alternatives to make up the difference. Alternatively, they may seek lower-cost homes or other housing options or avoid home ownership altogether, as many young people are doing today.[105]

Increasing costs for big purchases can keep them out of reach.

Those with access to lower-cost financing from the Family Bank are likely to be in a far more advantageous position financially than others in the future.

---

102   https://nces.ed.gov/programs/digest/d20/tables/dt20_330.10.asp?current=yes
103   Ibid.
104   https://www.attomdata.com/news/market-trends/home-sales-prices/attom-data-solutions-q4-2020-u-s-home-affordability-report/
105   https://www.investopedia.com/news/real-reasons-millennials-arent-buying-homes/

27.
STANDING THE TEST OF TIME

"The peace of the world has been preserved, not by the statesmen, but by the capitalists."

—Benjamin Disraeli[106]

WHEN GENGHIS KHAN was a little boy, he and his brothers reportedly fought constantly, to the distress of their mother. One day, she told them a tale of one of her ancestors, Alan Gua, whose five sons also quarreled regularly. According to legend, Alan Gua gathered them together and gave each of them an arrow and asked them to break it, which they all did with little effort. Then, tying five arrows together with string, she asked them to break the bundle of arrows. None could break or even bend the bundle of arrows. "Brothers who work separately," she said, "like a single arrow shaft, can be easily broken; but brothers who stand together against the world, like a bundle of arrows, cannot be broken."[107]

Families who invest in each other's success through the principles and practices of the Family Bank have the potential to enjoy greater unity than those who do not. Rather than succumb to the predictable divisiveness that most often accompanies heirs who receive inherited wealth, members of the Family Bank can

---

106 As quoted in Niall Ferguson, *The House of Rothschild, the World's Banker, 1849–1998, Vol. 2* (New York: Penguin Books, 1998).

107 http://www.mongolianculture.com/PaulaL-Sabloff.htm See also *Aesop's Fables*

enjoy the distinct honor of being a part of something greater that is intertwined with their family's history. Their access to financial education and future investment capital gives them remarkable opportunities for personal growth and community service. Family members will grow up recognizing that their heritage gives them greater responsibility to be good examples to others and good stewards of the wealth their family has accumulated. John D. Rockefeller's granddaughter, Ariana Rockefeller, once said of her family, "Grandpa really instilled in us that our family has the most strength when working together toward the greater good."[108]

Contrary to the opulent lifestyle of other millionaire and billionaire families, those who have access to a Family Bank tend to live more modestly. Parents teach their children the importance of money and charity without focusing on the wealth they can access. While attending school as a boy, David Rockefeller Jr. was surprised to hear some classmates discuss his family's significant wealth. "I didn't know my family was wealthy. I didn't personally feel rich, so I disagreed with them."[109] He credited his parents for not living luxuriously and demonstrating by example their respect for money. "I think it's very important that you not get used to going first class when you're a kid, because otherwise you don't learn the value of not having that. And I think that was part of the teaching. Our parents could have given us a lot more and we would have been spoiled and we would not have learned."[110]

In order to perpetuate the Family Bank beyond one or two

> *Family Bank families tend to live more modestly.*

---

108   https://www.ncfp.org/wp-content/uploads/2020/07/FinalCompressedDigitalPDF.pdf
109   https://www.cnbc.com/2018/04/16/how-david-rockefeller-jr-found-out-he-was-rich.html
110   Ibid.

generations, legal and financial plans must be established. Those who already own whole life insurance policies individually for their personal benefits may be able to transfer those policies into family trusts or other legal entities designed to make those funds available to descendants perpetually. The trusts and other entities must have flexible provisions allowing beneficiaries and successor trustees to be added later. Competent legal and tax advisors should guide you through those decisions.

> *Your family name can signify a commitment to success.*

To keep the Family Bank's principal funds available and growing perpetually, Family Banks should allocate and disperse funds appropriately. Parents and family members can easily continue the family's traditions that have made it so successful. Families with established Family Banks can share a sense of collective pride that they are unique in their community. Their last name should not suggest superiority, but it should remind them of their family commitment to pursue individual success and help others around them. They can best do this by actively sharing the perpetuation of their family's wealth and the sound principles of financial opportunity and responsibility that facilitated their individual prosperity.

With the right planning and commitment to nurturing the Family Bank perpetually, families will be able to beat the inheritance statistics. Members will be equipped with the knowledge, experience, and tools to achieve great financial and personal success thanks to their family's wise planning. This process may be repeated over and over, generation after generation, with the right structure and assets in place.

28.
THE ROAD AHEAD

"The empires of the future are the empires of the mind."

—Winston Churchill[111]

AMERICANS ENJOY A rich tradition of freedom and opportunity that sets us apart in world history. Few countries in the world have provided its citizens with as many advantages and as few limitations to personal freedom as the United States. Though we have our challenges—and the current social and economic difficulties may feel overwhelming—we have already seen unprecedented progress over the span of our lifetimes. The royal aristocrats of old never enjoyed the conveniences that ordinary, contemporary Americans regard as commonplace necessities today, such as electricity and indoor plumbing. And consider what technology alone has facilitated—greater access to information and education, health and medical advancements that improve health and extend lifespans, and new financial markets with innovative goods and services becoming more accessible to more people.

On the other hand, we also seem to be witnessing an unprecedented acceleration in natural, economic, social, military, and other calamities every year. The entire world has

We live in historically challenging times.

---

111   Speech at Harvard University, Cambridge, MA, Sept. 6, 1943.

recently been snarled by the COVID-19 pandemic, and this latest challenge has significantly strained our economy in addition to affecting most aspects of life. Millions of Americans who were laid off in the middle of the pandemic are still trying to climb out of unemployment and grapple with reduced incomes. Historically high inflation in 2021 and 2022,[112] projected by some to persist for several years, has further reduced the dollar's purchasing power and placed additional pressure on those with already limited or fixed incomes.

Examining the remarkable history of this country should give us hope. We have endured staggering difficulties stemming from the Civil War, World War I, the Great Depression, World War II, and many other natural, health, political, and military challenges. In each instance, we have soldiered on.

> *Catastrophes can facilitate unprecedented progress.*

Historically, pandemics and other catastrophes have subsequently led to greater progress and innovation. Perhaps the darkest time in human history occurred while the Black Plague, also called the Bubonic Plague, repeatedly struck Europe during the fourteenth century. The plague killed nearly half of the continent's inhabitants and significantly impacted medieval life in remarkable ways; it completely upended societal norms economically, politically, and even spiritually. Kings and Popes who were previously considered invincible and infallible were now susceptible to the same disease that was killing peasants and beggars. Widespread death caused a crisis of faith and fealty throughout the continent. Because the feudal system was so embedded in every facet of society in medieval Europe, it is unlikely that anything short of a major catastrophe like the plague could have overthrown it.

---

112 https://www.bls.gov/cpi/

As laborers started dying off by the thousands, demand for labor increased throughout Europe. Though most peasants had pledged fealty covenants to specific landowners as generations of their forebears had before, these "essential" workers began walking off the job for better prospects. Neighboring landowners competed for their hire by offering greater benefits of higher wages, improved housing, and better protection from roaming mercenaries who regularly sacked peasants' goods and livestock. Long disregarded as the lowest rung of the societal ladder, more and more peasants began owning property and amassing wealth.

As more people started owning more property, goods, and services, new markets for trade developed. Though commerce had hardly existed previously in the medieval world, a new merchant class emerged and became extraordinarily rich. The aristocracy, hemorrhaging money from empty fields and dwindling tax revenues, began intermarrying with merchant families to shore up their losses. "Pure" bloodlines became less valuable than coffers of gold, and certain merchant families who were born in obscurity suddenly found themselves kin with the rulers of Europe.

Dramatic changes in intellectual thought started to occur in the medieval world as well. While the dogmatic teachings of the Catholic church dominated the fields of philosophy and science for centuries in Europe, the church had few practical or spiritual answers for the cause and treatment of the plague. Some of the faithful increased their devotion in response to the plague, but much of society abandoned it. Everyday people found themselves questioning every assumption they had previously held because, in some cases, it became a matter of life and death.

An age of intellectual and scientific rebirth commonly labeled the *Renaissance* immediately followed the Black Plague's waning dominance. Ordinary people, liberated from the shackles of the dying feudal system, were living, working, and thinking better. Scientists such as Galileo emerged and encouraged others to discover the principles of natural law through personal experience rather than aristocratic or ecclesiastical instruction. These "Renaissance men" revealed the means of their easily repeated experiments and encouraged all to learn for themselves, and everyday people began discovering and testing natural law through personal and practical application. Humankind subsequently made significant scientific, social, and economic progress in a relatively brief time.

Today, a similar movement may be starting throughout the world. Recall how more and more people are conducting business right now—from their own homes. Digital innovations have removed traditional barriers in commerce, such as information and supply, among other things. This kind of interconnectivity is unprecedented, and information and commerce may become increasingly digitized and may even expand as a direct result of the COVID-19 outbreak. Because Americans have a habit of taking their destiny into their own hands by starting and expanding business enterprises, we may see even more entrepreneurs delivering innovative ideas and new services to the marketplace than ever before.

With billions of people receiving access to vaccines and becoming more aware of protective health practices, diseases worldwide may actually have a more limited effect on humankind going forward. Billions of people are now more conscious of the spread of disease, and medical advances such as vaccines and therapeutics are starting to prevent or greatly reduce the effects of infections of all kinds. As there are fewer victims of traditionally lethal diseases, there will be more people, more technology, more markets, and more progress.

Also consider what the COVID-19 pandemic has done for many families: they have chosen to spend more time together. Families are strengthening relationships and making more memories together. People are rediscovering that they actually like being around their families and are doing their best to work and play together. Families who spend more time together naturally become more invested in each other's happiness and success.

Besides preparing for future disasters, families must prepare for what may be one the greatest challenges in American history—an unprecedented transfer of wealth from more than 75 million "boomers"[113] primarily to their children and grandchildren. While it is unknown exactly how much wealth will be transferred, estimates are in the tens of trillions over the next two decades.[114] Families in the coming decades are likely to confront even greater difficulties associated with the "wealth riddle" proportional to the greater amount of wealth being transferred. All the financial and relationship problems that can result from traditional planning will be magnified by more money, and families will need to think differently to survive and thrive.

> *One of our greatest challenges is just around the corner.*

Families who plan ahead and establish Family Banks will have the tools to educate family members to be responsible and facilitate their financial independence. The Family Bank will be there to help bring wealth to its members in both good times and bad. Families are uniquely equipped to weather future crises and facilitate prosperity better than other institutions or groups. They know their members, care about them, and have a vested interest in their welfare and success. It's possible that in the midst of future calamities, government and charitable stopgaps may not be able to provide needed aid to everyone. Individuals and families may

---

[113] https://www.prb.org/resources/just-how-many-baby-boomers-are-there/

[114] https://www.cnbc.com/2021/07/12/the-great-wealth-transfer-has-a-big-tax-impact-how-to-reduce-the-bite.html

become the primary source of catastrophic assistance, and Family Banks may be able to help when others will not or cannot.

Greater discoveries and innovations await us. The Family Bank can help us find them.

Dreams coupled with hard work and tools can become reality through the Family Bank. We may have little comprehension of what remarkable innovations and progress lie ahead.

If the stories and ideas from this book have brought you a measure of clarity about the issues we have explored, I invite you to act. Don't let enlightening information simply provide a temporary delight like a marshmallow; seek out another course of nutritious food for thought and keep going. Act on the information you have received by consulting with your legal, tax, and financial professionals. Ask them for information about a Family Bank and whether it makes sense in your family. If they don't know what you're talking about, refer them to this book or find another professional who can help. Your family's and community's potential can be greatly enhanced by putting these ideas into practice, and future generations could benefit from your wisdom and generosity.

Thank you for reading this. I hope you have found it worthwhile. Spread the word and let's make some dreams come true for generations to come.

If you have any questions or would like additional insight, please feel free to contact the author via his website: www.tfbstrategies.com

www.ingramcontent.com/pod-product-compliance
Lightning Source LLC
LaVergne TN
LVHW041941070526
838199LV00051BA/2861